Love, Perversion
or Just Nature?

James Prince

Order this book online at www.trafford.com
or email orders@trafford.com

Most Trafford titles are also available at major online book retailers.

Printed in the United States of America.

ISBN: 978-1-4907-5276-1 (sc)
ISBN: 978-1-4907-5275-4 (e)

Scripture quotations marked KJV are from the Holy Bible, King James Version
(Authorized Version). First published in 1611. Quoted from the KJV Classic
Reference Bible, Copyright © 1983 by The Zondervan Corporation.

Trafford rev. 01/06/2015

www.trafford.com

North America & international
toll-free: 1 888 232 4444 (USA & Canada)
fax: 812 355 4082

CHAPTER 1

Today at age sixty-seven I ask myself this one question about the love experiences of my childhood.

Was it love, perversion or yet just nature when at age seven I wanted to make love to the young girlfriend of mine, the one I wanted as a wife?

She was my age; her name is Fernade, a young, gentle and pretty girl, for as much as I can remember. She was though also very stubborn and she allowed me to undress her, to watch her naked and to touch her where ever I wanted, but never to make love to her completely.

God knows that I tried with all of my heart and telling her that all the couples of the world were doing it; including her parents and mine. She repeated many times that we had to be married first.

Don't you ever think that a young boy of seven doesn't have any erection, because I had some that were very painful. Some people would say that I deserve it, I mean the pain.

I cannot tell where those profligate ideas came from either, because my parents were not demonstrative at all. In those days they hardly got undressed at all to make children. One day I heard my mom say this about my father: 'Nobody would be able to say that we are fooling around.' Poor woman that my mom was, I thought.

I remember telling one of my sisters who is a year older than me, meaning she was eight years old at the time when a young couple came to our place to tell us they were getting married and they just became engaged. When they kissed with the tip of their lips I told her then they were kind of dummies, because they weren't even using their tongue.

Where I got that? I have no idea. There was not even television in 1952. The only explanation I have today is that I had quite of an imagination then. To tell you the truth, this can be a precious trump for a writer. If only someone could have directed me in that direction when I was young; I could possibly have a hundred books written to my credit today.

Another thing I was a great user of in my childhood was for sure some embellishing. There is no doubt in my mind. I was often accused of lying when in fact I was only embellishing the stories. That was only to make them a little more interesting, especially the fighting stories.

To tell you the truth, I had hundreds of them, but I didn't lose too many, this said without embellishment. Embellishing is another important trump for a writer, no doubt.

Now, coming back to my love stories, if I can say, I just could play hide and seek with the other kids without thinking of finding a great place where I could hide with my beautiful girlfriend. I was looking for a place where no one could find us, but I have to say the risk to be found was quite high too, because the searcher wouldn't quit looking this easily. I have to say too that I never liked to be caught with my pants down, except by my girlfriend maybe.

When I think of it today, I found it strange that I never got caught or almost never; although maybe the reason why Fernande's father didn't like me too much was just because she told him what I did to her.

My two older sisters were guarding the house one day and they complained to him about me being a little brat. He came to get me and he made me travel from the first to the second story suspended to his arm, but this was done outside the railing and I got really scared.

It is very possible that my little girlfriend betrayed me and told her father about our activities. It is possible too that my behaviour that day was just because I wanted a chance to go upstairs to play with her. Although, I remember more my transportation to the second floor than my time spent with her. For sure that under the surveillance of the father we couldn't play hiding too much or else I would remember.

For sure too that I learned very young what was my sexual orientation and I never had any doubt about it. We were leaving in the area of Sudbury Ontario back then.

Before Fernande there was another pretty girl by the last name of Houle. She was certainly interested in me, because she followed me to the outhouse at school in the afternoon break. I can't really remember who followed who, her or me, but what I really remember is that we got caught naked. In fact it is the only time in my entire life that I got caught with my pants down. I clearly remember that we both enjoy the experience very much. I think it was worth the trouble, the penalty and the humiliation we had to live through afterwards.

I don't know what the consequences were for her later on, but one thing is sure, this never did discourage me from being attracted by the opposite sex.

When I think of it now, there was one more before these two girls and this was in the Abitibi region, precisely in Baraude. I was only six then, but now I can tell that I was quite precocious for my age. I remember I walked a very long way to get to her place to be with the little girl I was in love with and yet this was a region infested with four legs mean wolves. We had to barricade our house's door with everything we could put our hands on every night to stop them from reaching at us. Almost every night those wolves came to scratch at our door in a hope to reach us. We, all the kids were alone with our mother, because our father was in the bush trying to make enough money to put food on the table.

I didn't go back to see this girl, but it was not because of the wolves. The father of this pretty girl, name Gaudreau was quite strict and he had a very loud voice that brought down my libido very quickly. I kind of think now that her father remembered his childhood that was maybe very similar to mine, especially about sexuality.

Another thing I can say today with certainty is one of the dictum: 'Out of site, out of mind.' This could have been attributed to me then at least when it comes to my young love ones.

Things have changed since then though, because I'm in love with the same woman for more than fifteen years now. Her name is Sheba and this without being tormented by the sexual desire. I have received an answer to my prayer, the one which says; Deliver me from evil my Lord. Thank You my Lord. This inspired me of one song that is one of my favourite and it's called: The Smell of Roses, simply because of my taste for women and because the rose is the flower of love. I play it almost every day on my stereo for my Lord and it helps me going to sleep also.

Thank You my Lord, thank You my Lord, thank You my Lord.

1
Thank You my Lord for this wonderful smell of roses.
Thank You my Lord for giving me so many things.
Is it for us time of the apotheoses?
It's time for me to say thank You for great blessings.

I know You are the Almighty
You have made this beautiful flower just for me.
She is faded, as You can see.
Only You can bring her back to what she used to be.

We are the seed, the garden of your kingdom.
Your creation made by your hands, your ambition.
Your enemy, yes this despicable phantom
He has faded my nice flower, my companion.

God You blessed us and You told us. Genesis 1, 28.
To be fruitful, to multiply, fill up the earth.
To rule over, birds in the sky,
Fish in the sea and everything upon the earth.

Thank You my Lord for this wonderful smell of roses.
Thank You my Lord for giving me so many things.
Is it for us time of the apotheoses?
It's time for me to say thank You for great blessings.
Thank You my Lord for making me as your likeness.

It is a sure thing that to accomplish his will to fill up the earth, God needed to equip the human beings with the power; what it takes to reproduce just like every other animal on the face of the earth.

Some people don't want to believe in my love stories or I should say; in my sexual experiences of my childhood, but they have no problem believing that a young puppy dog of six months old could jump his mother in heat and this without even haven put a single leg at school.

Why wouldn't a young boy or a young girl have as much intelligence or a huge desire instinct of reproduction than a young dog? It is true though that a young dog has his sense of smelling way more developed than a child, but even so.

Some people have a hard time accepting that other people can be different. I remember having a hard time and I even got made at my mom, because she let my young brother walk around the house with her high heel shoes and her purse. It was obvious that he had a different sexual orientation than mine.

Are they born like this or do they become like this? This is a question that many people are still debating. I know for myself I was born as I am and that nobody made me a heterosexual; although I know too it is up to everyone to live or not our sexual life. I know too that today I would rather be castrated than to live in the abomination, which displeases my God. I know too that it is a strength that can only come from God.

There is only one recipe to do so and this is to love God more than ourselves, more than our sexuality, more than the religion, more than anything. This is something that is not given to everybody. This is the recipe Jesus gave us to obtain eternal life.

This is the greatest gift God has given me, my love for Him and this would explain why I was delivered from evil. This has nothing to do with my age either, because my erections are almost just as strong as they were in my young years, not so painful though.

It is not easy as we grow to understand what is right from what is wrong. There are a lot of things, for myself I did not understand before the age of seven. My own mother is a great jokes teller like many people, but just like I do, she can tell a dirty jokes not because it is dirty, but because it is funny. Although when a young kid listen to it and doesn't really understand the real sense of things, he or she makes his own mind and tell himself that if his mother, who is a good person can tell a story about sex, tails, breasts and vagina, the young boy that I was could play with them.

I remember telling a friend of mine a joke that I myself composed when I was in my thirties and it goes like this: What is a priest penis used for other than to pee? Of course I didn't pay attention of her three children who were watching the television and seem not to even care about the adult's conversation.

A few days later my friend second oldest boy came back from school laughing his head off. He asked his teacher who is a nun the same exact question.

Of course I was quite rushing asking him what the teacher's reaction was. He told us that she asked for the answer. I don't really know what she was expecting, but she told him this was a good one.

I was wondering myself why she was so anxious to know the answer, which is in French: Ça sers d'os. Which is pronounced like Sacerdoce, which is priesthood in English. Ça sers d'os, which means; used as a bone in English.

I kind of thought that this young boy was fairly precocious too! He sure paid attention to our conversation without letting us know about it.

Another thing I think might have been an important factor in my race for the sexual conquests in my childhood was the visit of a twelve years old boy; our neighbour who came to our place when my parents were out shopping for grocery. I don't remember exactly how he did it, but he managed to get my two oldest sisters and myself to put our pants down. I vaguely remember that it was a question of comparison. It sure was a good trick for him, because he got what he wanted. It was a good thing I was not too inhibited, I was only nine.

He was speaking English only and us not too much. This happened in a little community by the name of

South Stukely near Eastman in the East side of the province.

There again, if my two oldest sisters could get undressed by a young boy totally unknown to us; it meant in my little head that anything was allowed to me too. I probably understood very early too that if my parents had to hide to play those games, this is what I had to do too.

Some people asked me why the necessity to speak or to write about these sexual stories of my childhood. The answer is very simple. I heard on a very popular talk show this week on television an animator promoting homosexually. He is a homosexual himself and he asks his people to come out of the closet and to be proud of what they are. He seems to be very proud himself to be what he is. There are also many pride parades all over the country. I don't want in any case to promote sexuality at least to the youngsters, but I think the heterosexuals have the right to know too what the nature is all about. These youngsters must know and be warned of the danger coming from the adults of both sexes. They must know it is normal to be curious about both sexes, but it is not normal to be solicited by adults; no matter if they are from family or pure strangers.

I feel very sick to my stomach each time I hear on the news that a young child got kidnapped, knowing that for most of the time this was done by a sexual maniac, a paedophile. What scares me even more than this is the fact the authorities will use this reason to implant the microchips and this as early as childhood even maybe right from birth.

They will tell us this is done to find the lost children in cases of kidnapping and this will be accepted by the majority, but the real reason will be much different.

Another sexual predator just got caught lately in New York this time. A rich and well known Frenchman, which means he is very powerful. He could afford escorts women by the dozens and apparently he went to force himself on a maybe helpless chambermaid. This only proves one thing to me and that is the whole situation was beyond him. He couldn't help it.

Maybe I repeat myself, but it is more than due time that a pill is created to make the libido turn down a little bit for this kind of people. This guy himself should have thought about it for his own good and to avoid the shame on himself and on his own family and friends.

But, just like Jesus said: 'Woe to the world because of its stumbling blocks! For it is inevitable that stumbling blocks come, but woe to that man through whom the stumbling block comes.'

It's true that in moments like these, these men, men like this guy have more tail than brains. I'm sure too that he is not the first man to put his marriage in jeopardy and at risk this way and this was not the first time either. Not only he put his marriage at risk, but he also put an end to a prodigious and international career.

I don't really know it, but it seems to me that it would be harder on a very rich person to spend time behind bars than for a poor one. The poor one would at least get fed, maybe even better than at home, which would explain why so many youngsters do practically anything to get caught just before winter.

The question I ask myself now is this one: 'Did he have a childhood similar to mine or is he still at the same stage I was when I was seven; meaning practically unconscious and irresponsible for his actions?

What ever it is; this will cost him way more than it ever cost me and this is already a fact of life for him.

Another one, an archbishop who spent more than half of his life preaching in catholic churches just got caught promoting and dealing with infantile or juvenile pornography. How many people and mainly how many children he contaminated and mixed up in their little head of young kids before his arrest?

He would surely get a few years in jail, but one thousand years is not enough for such a crime. If he only gets one year for each person he scandalized, this could seem fair to me. This could easily be more than two thousand years. He is going to find out one day that God's justice is quite a bit fairer than men's justice.

One thing is sure and this is if he loved God more than anything and especially more than himself; he would have asked for help if he couldn't help himself.

There are thousands of cases like this one and I hope there are some among them who will have a chance to read this book of mine and they will use some of these advices for their own salvation. They'll have a much better chance to be brought to repentance if they really pay for their crime in this world instead of being hidden by their superiors.

I myself have never been approached by any adult except by a sixteen years old when I was twelve, but I settled the case myself and good for them too, because for sure I would have given them away.

As far as I can remember I always loved God, but I never wanted to be a church boy, which I believe saved me from bad misadventures with some of them. I remember going to the church basically every morning for a time, but this was because the young girl I liked was going there every day. She sure changed since and me too, but her apparently not for the better. We were seeing each other most of the time at the playground. She married my cousin, but it didn't work very long. According to the gossips she became quite wild. It's true that we change as we're getting older and this not always to be a better person.

This one I thought she was too good to even think about sex with her, poor her. I thought she was a saint. Maybe she was then. I think I had started my period of timidity and my period of uncontrollable shyness back then, which forbidden me from populating the earth in a way that I could dearly regret it today.

God has his own way to protect his children. So for the next six or seven years, during my puberty years, when I loved a girl, I was loving her silently. The only way I could tell her my love, it was in a song. I composed one hundred and sixty in French and eighty in English. I have to say too that many of them were for the same girl or the same woman.

My two first songs were for the same girl to whom I still think about quite often. Out of all the girls I have known, none of them has given me as many and none of them has given me such strong erections. She was never aware of it either. The ceiling and the walls of my bedroom were the ones which paid the price. She had the most beautiful eyes in the world. Her big eyes called for names and one of them was owl, which was not too flattering, but to me she was the most beautiful. She also developed a very nice pair of round breasts as early as twelve years old. I was dreaming of them days and nights. I never realized until now, but I'm sure that I had dozens of fights with other boys in my village because of her. I'm sure now that I think of it that many boys who were also interested in her fought me because I loved her and because I was always at her place.

She is also the main reason why I still miss a piece of my thumb. I was splitting wood to make kindling to light up the stove in the morning very often at thirty degrees below in the house. I cut them in a way that when I put the light to it, it started right away, so I could return to my bed before I freeze my ass.

Liette basically never came my side, but she did it that day and when my young sister who was bringing the kindling inside the house saw her; she mentioned to me the one I loved was getting close to us. I lifted my head, but the axe was already on the way down and my thumb was still on the piece of wood.

My young sister started screaming right away: 'Your thumb, your thumb.' I then asked her what was wrong with my thumb. She said, 'It's on the ground.'

I don't know what you think of the whole story, but I can tell you that cutting a finger, the bone included; this kind of things makes an erection of a young boy go down very quickly. Instead of having the chance to have a joyful meeting with the girl I loved with all of my heart; I had to wrap my hand in a towel and rush to the hospital. By the time I got there, I had barely any blood left. It hurts twice as much and it hurts for a long time.

My first song is called: When We Only See One Star. It's not made in English, but I'll translate it for you.

When we only see one star there in the skies
We have to set sail, because it's a great spring.
When you say you love me I believe I'm in heaven
I feel the real poem of your real love.

When we love each other for real
We say sweetheart I'll love you forever
When we only see one star there in the skies,
This is happiness
You have to lift your up your veil,
Because I have given you my heart.

I was only thirteen when I composed this one. I composed another one a year later and it's called: Liette and this one is not written in English yet either. It's on a fiddle tune, but I don't know the name of it.

Liette
Liette my sweet love, I will always love you
I want you to be mine, to love me, to be with me
My darling I also want you to be happy with me together
If you want to be.
By myself I'm bored to death,
With you everything shines.
When I'll see you again come and kiss me sweet
I would love to hold you for all the times I couldn't.

My father who was one of the best fiddlers in the country has never left me forget this one. It is a nice tune that he particularly likes and every time he wanted to play it and he couldn't remember it, he asked me to hum it.

The destiny is made of many strange little things; nevertheless, my composer career was started.

These two songs for sure were more of their time in the fifties than they are now, but I still like the songs, the tune and the girl, which brings me to a more recent song this time and it's called: I Never Quit Loving.

I Never Quit Loving
No I never quit loving
The girls who have been by my side.
I'm a guy who gives everything.
Some of them took me for a ride
I never forgot by first love
Even though I was only six
But it's not often I think of
The one who chased me with a stick.
Chorus

Maybe there's someone to tell me.
What have I done? For they're all gone.
I am helpful and I'm faithful
And more I never quit loving
2
I met some blonds, some with dark hair,
Even a red longtime ago.
I always try hard to be fair.
It is the only way I know.
I have counted many failures.
It is not fun, but amazing.
That despite all those adventures,
Through all I never quit loving.
Chorus
Maybe there's someone to tell me.
What have I done? For they're all gone.
I am helpful and I'm faithful
And more I never quit loving
3
Now I'm ready to retire,
What's my hope after all those years?
I am still hot as a fire
And never been afraid of tears.
And I'm not scared to give my heart
To the one I've been looking for.
I know she will be my sweetheart
And I will never look for more.
Chorus
Maybe there's someone to tell me.
What have I done? For they're all gone.
I am helpful and I'm faithful
And more I never quit loving
1-4
No I never quit loving
The girls who have been by my side.

I'm a guy who gives everything.
Some of them took me for a ride
I never forgot by first love
Even though I was only six
But it's not often I think of
The one who chased me with a stick.
Chorus
Maybe there's someone to tell me.
What have I done? For they're all gone.
I am helpful and I'm faithful
And more I never quit loving.
Ho no I'll never quit loving.

Who knows? Maybe it is because I never quit loving, even my first girlfriend that my adult relationships didn't work too well.

Although I think it is never wrong to love, I mean really love. We can love someone without thinking of slipping with this someone. I always loved Liette and I never slept with her and I never thought of her sexually once I heard she was married either and I still love her. We can love someone without always thinking about this person. We can still love the ex girlfriends without cheating on the one we are with and without committing adultery in our heart.

Many of the jealous people wish their partners would lose their memories about their ex relationships. I think it is a very strange way to love someone, but it is not my way at all. To love someone is or should be to make this someone happy and jealousy does the exact opposite. I am single now for the last fifteen years and I sincerely believe that God allows it this way to allow me to write what He wants me to tell, the truth, his word to the world.

'Go and make disciples of all nations.' This means to make the truth known across the world. The truth the church's leaders have hidden from you. It is written in Matthew 28, 19-20.

Maybe you would ask me why then all of my sexual stories. Well, because just like in the time of Noah, most of the world population is more incline to listen to the sex stories, the stories of ass and breasts than to listen to the word of God. So it takes what it takes to get people to listen and in my case to read what I have to say. Go read what it's written in Matthew 24, 38, which is very similar to what we are seeing today.

'For as in those days before the flood they were eating and drinking, marrying and giving in marriage, until the day that Noah entered the ark and they did not understand until the flood came and took them all away, so will the coming of the son of man be.'

We don't talk about marry your daughter you do well and don't marry her you do better here, but about fathers who sleep with their daughters. Men who need a pill to reduce their libido like I was talking about earlier.

Either we like it or not, sex is a great part of normal life, at least for normal people. The whole human race is equipped with it. This is the way God, the Creator made us. He made us to his image, which means with whatever it takes to procreate too.

For this to happen it takes a male and a female who do what they have to do to breed with their personal equipment. There is absolutely nothing dirty at all about this and as you should all know; those instruments are made to go one into the other. I figured it out by myself when I was only six. This is not a caramel chocolate bar and neither a bubble gum mystery.

All the rest, especially sodomy is nothing else than abomination, according to the word of God that was given to us through the prophets. It is written in Leviticus

18, 22 among others. 'You shall not lie with a male as one lies with a female, it is an abomination.'

Note too that adultery among heterosexuals is also an abomination. It is just as bad as sodomy and not less as scandalous. This said to the ones who judge others without looking at themselves.

Why do I talk about this? It's because we cannot count on paedophile and homosexual priests to do it. During the dozen years I went to church; I never ever heard a priest even once talked about this and yet this is about the whole foundation of the world, God's creation. They don't preach against their own parish.

There was a referendum at the Catholic Church were my oldest sister goes. This was to find out if the homosexual priest should stay or leave. They voted for him to stay. I imagine it would be easier for the ones like him to go confess their sins. They have a better chance to be understood this way, poor them.

CHAPTER 2

From the age of eleven to the age of sixteen I was madly in love with Liette. I still cannot understand to this day the patience her parents had with me. I was at her place almost every weekend and this from seven o'clock till two in the morning when the television station was closing down. There were two good reasons for me, 1; I was going away from my home, 2; I was much closer to the one I was in love with. My friend, her brother was telling me to shut everything down before leaving when he left me to go to sleep.

Her father was very strict with all of his children. I have seen him a couple of times in fits and let me tell you; it was not pretty at all. No point saying that he was respected by all of them, but then, why so much patience with me? This is something I would have loved to know before they passed away and I might never know. I know one thing and this is I would have never allowed it in my house.

I didn't give a heck about the television or any of the programs that were on it. I have seen myself hundreds of times though in imagination getting up and joining Liette in her big bed once everyone else was asleep. I was an exceptional scene maker. I would have surely got killed by her father or at least been kicked out the door if he ever caught me this way with her daughter. She might have pulled my eyes off too, if I went to see her in the middle of the night without telling her beforehand and have her approval.

The fact was that I loved her way too much to risk losing her with a bad move, but she wouldn't have had to ask me twice. I took her out only once to watch a couple of movies at the theatre. During the three hours we spent together, which is from the time I picked up and the time I drop her at her place I said two words. Those words were hi when I arrived and bye when I left. When you are prisoner of your timidity like I was; you're stuck and it's not funny. I was so afraid to make a mistake with her that I made the irreparable one.

I made another song about this and it's called: Prisoner of My Shyness.

I was prisoner of my shyness
I was prisoner of myself
How many girls I let go?
Some I could love and I know.
Some were sweet and sincere
And have everything to please me
But because I was too scared
Unwillingly I set them free.
I was too self-conscious,
Afraid that they laugh at me
Though I was ridiculous
And I was too blind to see
But now watch for yourselves ladies
Be careful for your own heart
Now I claim what I lost from these
I lost a lot from my sweethearts
I was prisoner of my shyness
I was prisoner of myself
How many girls I let go?
Some I could love and I know.

I am persuaded to this day that no one desired her as much as I did, as many times and in such intensive way. Knowing the sexual desire of a man drop by fifty per cent after ten years of marriage and that another twenty-five per cent drop again when he reach sixty; which totalize maybe seven thousand times the desire of a man for the same woman in fifty years. I think I have desired Liette more often than this. I have desired her intensively at least four times a day and every day during five years long; which would make seven thousand three hundred times. Believe me, I don't exaggerate at all and this is not counting all the other times in the rest of my life.

One thing though, in those days there were no birth-control pills and if it wasn't for my shyness, I would surely have started very young making babies. For sure I was not lacking the desire.

I was sixteen when her older brother came to Granby to tell me she was getting married shortly. I think she was only fourteen or fifteen at the time. I still don't know if the decision to tell me came from her or him, but either way, I appreciated the courtesy. I was though certainly not in a position to compete with any one at that age, especially about marriage and it was mostly my fault if she lost interest in me too. Another thing is sure is that I cried and I cried for a long time. I most likely shed as many tears for her as I had erections thinking about her. It's not the same kind of pain, but I didn't cry as much when I cut my finger. Although the only fact someone in her family came to tell me about her marriage meant she new I loved her. I never blame her in anyway. I loved her and this didn't mean she had to love me. The fact that I write about her today means and proves I always kept a large room in my heart for her. No I never quit loving.

There are a few things in the Bible which make me wonder for quite a few years now and it is written in Proverbs 5, 18 through 5, 20. 'Let your fountain be blessed, and rejoice in the wife of your youth, as a loving hind and a graceful doe, let her breast satisfy you at all times; be exhilarated always with her love. For why should you my son, be exhilarated with an adulteress and embrace the bosom of a foreigner?'

As you can see we can find sexual expressions in the Bible too. I'm pretty sure the original saying was; 'Suck the breast of a foreigner.' I have very often seen myself sucking the breasts of this young lady of my youth by the name of Liette, at least in my mind.

Some evil forces though have contributed to send me away from her. Only God knows the answer or the reason why; unless he told his angels about it and I'm pretty sure the devil has a good idea about it too. Although I know too that to get to the point where I'm today with my knowledge of the truth; I had to go through everything I went through.

This also means that God wants Liette to find out about it too; otherwise He wouldn't have inspired me to write this book and especially write about her. I do have a precise goal in life now and this is to touch as many people as possible and mainly the ones I love; even the ones who don't want to hear about the truth. Jesus told his disciples, the ones like me who listen to him, that we will be hated by all because of his name. This means by all who don't love God, the truth of course. It is written in Matthew 10, 22.

Let me tell you that there are already many pastors who don't like me or I should say; they don't like what I am doing. The more their churches will get empty, the more my life will be in danger, but I don't care about this, because according to Jesus the very hairs of my head are all numbered. See Matthew 10, 30.

For sure they are going to try to make me look like a fool first before trying to kill me; just like they did with Jesus and Louis Riel. By observing what they did in the pass we learn to know what they're going to do in the future and the way they are operating.

Just like Jesus, Louis Riel became not only very visible, but he also became a bit too influential and just like what happened with Jesus; there were a bit too many people who were following him, according to the authorities anyway. In both of these cases they managed to accuse them for crimes deserving death and in both cases they managed to kill them.

So this means I have a bit of time left, because I'm not too influential yet, since my own family refuse to follow me or to listen, which means I didn't become too dangerous for the organized church and the organized crime yet.

Nevertheless, the devil is always at work and let me show you an evident proof of it.

Remember the story of what happened in the Garden of Eden with Adam and Eve. God told them not to touch or to eat from the tree of the middle of the garden and if they were going to do it, certainly they would die. Then the devil came to tell them that they wouldn't die, but they will become like God, that their eyes will open, meaning they will know right from wrong. Adam and Eve didn't die physically, but they died spiritually, which the devil was too evil to tell them.

Now, many years later Jesus, the son of God came to tell us that not the least stroke of a pen will disappear from the law of God for as long as the earth and heaven will exist. You can read it in Matthew 5, 17-18. One more time the devil showed up and came to say the exact opposite.

See Ephesians 2, 15. 'By abolishing in his flesh the enmity, which is the Law of commandments contained in ordinances, so that in himself he might make the two into one man, thus establishing peace.

Look now at Romans 6, 13-14: 'For until the Law, sin was in the world, but sin is not imputed when there is no law. Romans 6, 14. 'For sin shall not be master over you, for you are not under the law but under grace.'

The devil, the lawless one can say all he wants, that there is no more law, the fact is the law will always be there. Paul said the sin is not imputed when there is no law, but basically all Christians say they all have sin. What kind of grace is this? That too they learned from Paul. Although by saying this they all are admitting they are the children of the devil. So, now you can see how the devil works.

God says one thing and the devil says the opposite. Jesus says one thing and Paul says the opposite.

I just hope you wouldn't take this information too lightly, because your salvation depends on it. Paul said in Ephesians 2, 15 as I underlined earlier that Jesus has established peace and yet Jesus himself when he came told us quite differently. You can read it in Matthew 10, 34. 'Do not think that I came to bring peace on earth, I did not come to bring peace, but a sword.'

And one more time among many others Paul says the exact opposite than Jesus. He contradicted Jesus not only once in a verse, but twice in the same verse. The one who was described as the lawless one in the Bible is the devil himself.

I composed a hymn, which speaks about it quite a bit called: Jesus' Messages.

'Just remember longtime ago
In my journey into this world.
I told you everything I know
About my Father's Holy Word.

That I didn't come to abolish
Neither the law or the prophets
And until all is accomplished
Everything stands don't you forget. Matthew 5, 17-18.
2
I said not the smallest letter
And not the least stroke of a pen
None from the law of my Father
Will disappear, so understand, (Matthew 5, 17-18.)
But what did tell you the liar?
That with my flesh unto the cross.
I destroyed law and barrier,
Rules and commandments for the lost. (Ephesians 2, 14-16.)
3
One asked me what was the greatest
Of the commandments in the Law. (Matthew 22, 25-36)
It was just to put me to test;
He tried to find in me a flaw.
Love your God with all of your heart,
With all your soul and all your mind. (Matthew 22, 37)
From your neighbour don't be apart,
Follow those two and you'll be mine. (Matthew 22, 39,
and Matthew 12, 50)
4
But what did tell you the liar?
That the whole Law is one command. (Galatians 5, 14)
And this is to love your neighbour
As yourself see now where he stands.
Doesn't speak about my Farther,
Cause sinners too love who loves them. (Matthew 5, 46)
It's good to love one another,
But this won't get to heaven.
5
Who's my mother? Who's my brother?
Who are my sisters and my friends? (Matthew 12, 48-50.)

He does the will of my Father,
My Father who is heaven
You are the salt of all the earth,
You are the light cause you believe. (Matthew 5, 13-14.)
Even though sometimes you get hurt,
Watch out for the one who deceives. (Matthew 16, 24 and 24, 4)
6
Like sheep I sent you in the field
Through wolves so be careful for your sake. (Matthew 10, 16.)
And like doves have God for your shield,
So therefore be shrewd as snakes. (Matthew 10, 16)
He is clever the enemy
In manipulating the truth
He is more crafty than any,
See he made Eve pick up the fruit.
7
So you will have for enemy
For sure members of your own house. (Matthew 10, 36.)
You will be not worthy of me
Not if you love more someone else. (Matthew 19, 37.)
To the earth then I brought the sword,
So take you cross and follow me. (Matthew 10, 34 and Matthew 16, 24.)
You won't be worthy of the Lord
If you put first your family. (Matthew 10, 37.)
8
I'm the one who sowed the good seed;
They are the sons of the kingdom. (Matthew 13, 38.)
My enemy who sowed the weeds
And they all are the devil sons. (Matthew 10, 39.)
One day I will send my angels
To throw the weeds in the furnace. (Matthew 13, 42.)
There will be then no more rebels,

You'll shine like the sun in this place. (Matthew 13, 43.)
1-9
Just remember longtime ago
In my journey into this world.
I told you everything I know
About my Father's Holy Word.
That I didn't come to abolish,
Neither the law or the prophets
And until all is accomplished,
Everything stands don't you forget.'
Everything stands don't you forget.' Matthew 5, 17-18.

Now people, you have to know and to realize that it's not Jesus who created the religions, because he was completely against this sordid slavery. You only have to read Matthew 23, 9 to be convinced of it and if this is not enough for you, I will show you a lot more. It is not God either, the One who put his word in the mouth of his servant, neither of the two wanted this hierarchy of popes, archbishops, bishops, cardinals, deacons, pastors and priests, who are false fathers.

If you read very carefully, you will see that it is this same lawless one who created the seven churches and that Jesus, the son of God only created one church, him who didn't have a place to rest his head. If Jesus wanted to, he could build a lot of churches, him who was a carpenter, because he would have got a lot of help with the four and five thousand men who were following him everywhere. The church Jesus created, the church he wanted has no wall and no roof. The church of Jesus is the truth, the word of God in our hearts.

Look at Matthew 4, 4 where Jesus said: 'Man shall not live on bread alone, but on every word that proceeds out of the mouth of God.'

Getting back to the lawless now (Paul) and being very careful at what we read, like Jesus recommended us to do like we can read in Matthew 24, 15, we can see that Paul's fake conversion is full of lies.

See Acts 9, 7. 'The men who travelled with him stood speechless, hearing the voice but seeing no one.'

Now look at the story told by the liar himself in Acts 22, 9. 'And those who were with me saw the light, to be sure, but did not hear the voice of the one who was speaking to me.'

Most of us know what the problem of the liars is, isn't it? They all end up getting mixed up with their lies. Jesus said that we will recognize the tree by its fruits, the liar by his lies. He also said that the devil was the father of lies.

You who read until now; you are warned and it is up to you from now on to pay attention, to be careful of what you're reading and mainly how you read like Jesus said in Matthew 24, 15. 'The reader will understand.' The French version says: 'Be careful when you read.'

Now in Jesus' time when they were talking about the writing, they were talking about the Scripture, the Old Testament, the Bible.

In the same verse Jesus mentioned the abomination in the holy place, which I think means the lies in the holy book. It is written at the beginning of every Bible that it is holy.

Coming back to sex, we have to understand that it was created by God and that it was his purpose and his goal to populate the earth and it was most likely to get a minimum of souls, a certain number who adore Him; meaning who love Him with all of their heart. Remember it is written: 'Many are called, but very few are chosen.' Matthew 22, 14.

The second God commandment, at the beginning, God said to Adam and Eve and I quote: 'Be fruitful and multiply, and fill the earth.'

Then after cleaning up the earth of its abominations with the flood; God repeated the same words to Noah and his family. That we want it or not, sex is the main instrument we need to make this happened and there are a lot of good people who are born from lazy parents.

Today we have sperm banks and clone. The fact is that there are from nine to twelve women for a man in the world; which means that for every couple of homosexuals there are at least another eighteen women who cannot find a man.

What should they do other than what they're doing these days? A lot of them become prostitutes and others are flirting with the other women's husbands and boyfriends. Most of the time, mainly the prettiest and the most sensual get what they're after, meaning love and sex, which causes adultery in profusion. Which also incites what we are experiencing in the world nowadays and this is a percentage of divorces of over sixty-six, a level probably never reach before.

Nevertheless, the downfall and the calamity don't stop here. Many children are abandoned either by one parent or by the other and very often by both. Very often too the children find themselves having two fathers and two mothers, which cause a lot of frictions within the members of a same family. It won't be surprising in a near future to see the children approving the death or the assisted suicide of their parents. They will probably pretend mercy and compassion and they will sign their consent. On the other hand, they will most likely change their mind if they are told they will lose their inheritance if they do.

One way or the other; it will be by indifference or even by revenge that the children will get rid of their parents. It is written that the love of the most will cool off.

See Matthew 24, 12. 'Because lawlessness is increased, most people's love will grow cold.'

Jesus said it and you can and you should believe it.

Parents will do the same thing with their disrespectful and full of hatred children. Jesus warned us about it too. See Matthew 10, 35-36. 'For I came to set a man against his father, a daughter against her mother and a daughter-in-law against her mother-in-law; and a man's enemies will be the members of his own household.'

It is not that Jesus wanted that the members of the same family fight among themselves, but he knew that within the same family it would be one out of two who believes the truth and the other one believes in the lies. I don't want to scare anyone, but let me tell you that we have reach this point. I can even tell you that right now; there are more members of my big family who believe in lies than the other way around and this even if I've been trying to let them know Jesus' messages for more than fifteen years like I'm doing right now in this book of mine. Yet, they all pretend to love God. I can tell you too that it is not an easy task for a Jesus' disciple. Although, I have to remember another message from Jesus who told me not to insist with these kind of people. See Matthew 10, 14. 'Whoever does not receive you or listen to your words, as you go out of that house or that city, shake the dust off your feet.'

But it is not this easy to abandon people we love to their very sad fate or to walk out of the house of your loved mother. It is also written that a prophet is not welcome in his own family and neither is a Jesus' disciple. What to do then? My only hope now is this book of mine will succeed in making a lot of disciples of all nations and one day one of them with I hope more influence than mine will be able to make them reflect and understand that all I do is for their own salvation. You see, it is written that if they perish it is just because they refuse to believe in the truth. See 2 Thessalonians 2, 10. 'And with all the deception of wickedness for those who perish, because they did not receive the love of the truth so as to be saved.'

So as you can see, the truth is very important and we can hardly get the truth without having love for it. To shut the door down on the truth is to shut down the door on your salvation. Nothing is simpler than this. Jesus said; Matthew 12, 30. 'He who is not with me is against me and he who does not gather with me scatters.'

This means you only have two choices. I made mine, which is yours? I made a song that I really like and it's called:

On Which Side Are You?

Will you be on the side of Jesus?
Will you be on the side of the one?
Who sacrificed his life so we can get a life;
The one who tells the truth that hid from you the enemy?
Will you be on the side of Jesus?
Will you be on the side of the one?
Who was killed on the cross,
The one that we can trust?
He gave his life for you;
All what he said is true, not like the enemy.
Will you be on the side of Jesus?
Will you be on the side of the one?
Who made you the promise, you will see liveliness
When you will be accused and
Then you won't be confused by the enemy?
Will you be on the side of Jesus?
Will you be on the side of the one?
Who said to be careful when the beast will be awful;
You will have to flee away

When you are persecuted by the enemy?
Will you be on the side of Jesus?
Will you be on the side of the one?
When he'll come back to get
All the ones who didn't forget,
The ones he'll put on his right,
On the other side his enemy
I know that I am on Jesus' side
I know I'm on the side of the one;
The one who told me the truth,
He was killed for the same truth,
But we'll win over the enemy.
Yes I am on the side of Jesus.

If you are on the Jesus' side you will help me to gather with me on the account of Jesus and this at the risk of your own life, but yet being shrewd as snakes and as innocent as doves. See Matthew 10, 16. 'Behold said Jesus; I send you as sheep in the mist of wolves; so be shrewd as serpents and as innocent as doves.'

Now what does this mean? It means exactly that you shouldn't go throw yourself in the mouth of the wolf. Don't you go and do what Louis Riel did. He died very young for trying to bring the truth from God to his friends, the priests, bishops and archbishops, those men who didn't really want the truth to be known and spread out. These same men who did everything in their power to make Louis Riel a mental case, but to be able to judge him and condemn him to death he had to be sound in body and mind.

It is fine to die for the cause of God, which is also the cause of Jesus and of Louis Riel, but you sure can talk to many more people if you are shrewd as snakes and simple as doves and if you stay alive. Don't you try to get kill on purpose. I don't think this would please God at all.

Apparently one warned man is worth two, so this is giving you a light advantage on your enemies. Louis Riel most likely thought his supposedly friends would love the truth as he did, but it was not the case.

I did try to convince them too and this for a short time, but luckily for me I quickly understood before it was too late that the truth wasn't welcome in Christian churches and neither was I with my knowledge. Just know this is an extreme luck if this book made it up to your hands; I would even say it is close to a miracle, because many people would do anything they can to stop it.

Four pastors from the Baptist Evangelist Church who seem to be quite friendly with me and some with whom I even hunted the big game turned on me as soon as they heard about my discovery of what I call the biggest scandal of all times, which are; the religions.

One of them went as far as putting down Matthew; one of the most credible Jesus' apostles saying that he was nothing but a vulgar tax collector, a publican who was working for the Romans. I said yes, he was a tax collector who left everything behind to follow Jesus; him who had nothing else to do than sitting down and pick up people's money to make a good living and to get rich and yet; Matthew left everything behind to follow Jesus, the master, something none of these false preacher could do. Matthew knew he just found a pearl of great value, the kingdom of heaven.

When Jesus says they are blinds who lead other blinds, he was telling the truth as usual. There is a very strong reason for them wanting to hide the truth; it is because the truth condemns them all from one end to the other, from the youngest to the oldest.

Jesus said it in Matthew 23, 15. 'Woe to you, scribes and Pharisees, hypocrites, because you travel around on sea and land to make one proselyte and when he becomes one, you make him twice as much a son of hell as yourselves.'

They make proselytes out of new born babies even before they have their eyes opened.

We learn a lot when we pay attention at what we read, especially in the Bible. This is a huge warning from Jesus that thousands, millions and billions of people unfortunately didn't take seriously enough since it was written. On the contrary, we were always told that everything written in the Bible was nothing but the pure truth, but it is the truth about the lies as well, the weeds spoken by Jesus.

Of course it is in the nature of things too that a male fights to gain the heart of the girl or the heart of the woman he loves. All the bucks of the deer family do it and I'm not sure, but I think that all males do it soon or later. My mother had to come to school up to seven times a day because of my fights in the school yard. There were many times I think that fights were directly caused because of my affection or my love for Liette. I must be a little slow, because I just realized it for the very first time; I mean the reasons for fighting.

Antonio and his brother Adrian along with Leo, one of Liette's brother best friends were waiting for me one day after school. When they told me they were going to beat me up, I didn't waste a single second and I kicked Leo just between the legs and I can assure you that I didn't miss. Then I jumped on Antonio with a good headlock grip while I was holding Adrian back with my legs. I didn't know then, but the school director was watching everything from a distance. We were all in the street near the schoolyard. The director then came to get Leo and me, since we were both students of that school, but he had no jurisdiction on the other two, whom I think had either quit or were thrown out of the school. Either way, me and Leo earned the right to get the regular punishment, which is the six strikes of the heavy strap when I suddenly burst out laughing after I got mine. I had my head bent down a little when I saw beside me the floor getting wet even before Leo got any strike. The pouring came from his eyes and his pants.

My mother asked if the authorities couldn't do anything to stop those fights, fearing that I could get hurt very bad one day. The director simply told her not to worry about me, that I was able to defend myself. I had many fights against Antonio and Adrian at the same time and twice against Antonio, Adrian and Emile, one of their older brothers. No one can say that these guys didn't hold on to each other, that's for sure.

When I think about it today though, I remember that Antonio got to be called an owl too, just like Liette. It was most likely because he too had an eye on her and this would explain why so many fights between me and them. No matter what it was, my departure from this village is most likely the reason why a drama was aborted. I often told myself that if I'd stayed there I would have had to kill one of them to save my life or I would have got killed by one of them. Twice their older brother, Raoul came to my defense calling his brothers cowards for getting three against a little guy like me who was smaller than any of them. I think that Raoul liked my older sister quite a bit; this said without wanted to discredit him in any way.

I don't remember looking for fights personally, but I know I never did too much to avoid them either. If someone was looking for me he could find me. The very last time I had troubles with them I was not living in this village anymore, but I was visiting. This was in the pull room that I was babysitting along with the owner's son. His parents were gone dancing along with my parents. They were again the three brothers, Antonio, Adrian and

Emile who decided it was time for me to pay for all the times they couldn't do it. I lifted up the oldest and I threw him on top of a pile of crates of empty pop bottles. Then I grabbed Antonio and I held him with his back against a pull table and I pushed as hard as I could holding the pull table bank while Adrian was punching me in my back until he started begging me to let go of his brother, because he was getting blue by the seconds and he thought he was dying. He must have had a sore back for a while. During all of that time I was scared to be hit on the head with a ball. It was for them probably just a way to make fun, but this was a fun that could have turn out to be a tragedy.

When our parents were back, my father was almost drunk and he was furious against them, but I was not there anymore. These same three brothers also attacked Clément, Liette's brother and this with an axe and whips, but as soon as the axe was pulled out of their hands and thrown in the field the whips were used against themselves and this for at least a mile long. It is useless to say that these guys were looking for troubles just about anywhere.

It is not easy either to figure out why so many others were looking for me all the time. One thing is sure is I had a lot of fights without looking for them and most of the time I was only defending myself. Maybe what caused this phenomenon was the fact my dad put me to work in the wood since I was only eleven and I became back then way stronger for my age than other kids my age did. I should indeed have had enough money to take a girlfriend out or to play pull, but I was not paid for the work I was doing even though I largely deserved it.

Nevertheless, the only fact I beat a boy way bigger and taller than me surely contributed to make other kids curious and wanted to try me. It was a kind of question to find out for themselves. Some of them suffered the experience with sore jaw and sore teeth.

Maybe it was too the fact I won a fight against three guys who were older than me and another one against five at the ice rink and another one against seven contributed to excite the curiosity of a few of them. If you are in good shape enough and you can beat three, you can also beat seven, because only three can get to you at the same time.

But as you probably know; there is a reason for everything and I am pretty sure that all of these fights have contributed to prepare me to become The Masked Defender that I am. To know more about this story; you will have to read my first book called: The Precious Princess of Wonderland.

One thing is sure; we need to know how to fight to engage in a fight against the devil and his lies. Although, I think it will be a fight of words for most of it, at least until his demons try to eliminate me.

What ever it is, I think God has started to train me for this fight since I was a little boy. For as long as I can remember I was always against injustice either it was directed against me or the others. The injustices against me from my own dad among others have caused many fights between us. During the school summers holidays he hired many kids and two of them were Liette's brothers who would surely recognize themselves when they read this book of mine.

We were six and at times seven youngsters from age eleven that I was through sixteen for the oldest. Not a single time, not a single day one of them succeeded to beat me in production and God knows and so does my mom that they all tried with the energy of despair. It was not a question of money, but a real question of pride for everyone. Back home on the Saturday afternoon it was payday. Of course dad was paying all the youngsters from fifteen dollars to twenty-five according to the production of everyone of them, but when it was my turn; me who had the biggest production of all, I was told he had no more change left.

There is a good reason why today; after all those years of frustrations, I simply cannot put up with any kind of injustices.

It is probably why when God showed me the way Paul took so much room, at least ninety-five per cent of the New Testament; I had an instant reaction. Paul who didn't spent a single minute with Jesus. One of my main goals, my greatest wish today would be to hear the testimonies of all the other apostles who actually spent time with Jesus, the Messiah.

We do have barely anything from Peter and yet he was the most considerate of all the apostles and if it wasn't for Matthew in the Bible; we would be almost in the dark when it comes to the truth. Jesus told us that Satan is a murderer and the father of lies from the beginning.

The Jesus' message, which reassure me the most is his last one when he told us that he will be with us until the end of ages. See Matthew 28, 20. This message is actually telling us that the truth, the word of God will always be with us. The reason is very simple I think; it is just because the beast actually needs the word of God and always did to operate his business, the churches, the religions and everything that goes with them. Jesus knew it.

I would like now to show you a few verses which demonstrate who they are and this right here in the Bible. Those are the things we find when we pay attention at what we read or the way we read. Not only they are murderers, but they are actually using your faith to kill.

Quite a challenge, I would say and only the devil and his angels are evil and crafty enough to do such things.

We already saw that Paul was killing Jesus' disciples in big numbers, but very few people know that this has never stopped. There are many ways to kill people, as you already know, but then there are more ingenious ways to do it. What would you say if some supposedly apostles would use the faith of the greatest believers to do it?

I asked a pastor from the Seven Day Adventist Church once if he was married and if he had any children. He said yes in both cases. I then asked him if his children truly believe in God. 'Of course!' He answered. I asked him then if he would give to his children or to any member of his congregation a poisoned lemonade to drink or else put in their hands a venomous snake or yet a scorpion. 'Of course not!' He said. Well, I said to him, Mark, Luke and Paul did it. 'Come on now!' He said. Take the Bible in Mark 16, 17-18 and read, would you?"

" 'These signs will accompany those who have believed; in my name they will cast out demons, they will speak new tongues; they will pick up snakes with their hands and when they drink any deadly poison, it will not hurt them. They will lay hands on the sick and they will recover.' "

What an abomination this is and how many believers do you think they have killed this way? I suppose many blind believers who believe blindly in these lies and in these liars tried this satanic supposition.

"Take a look now in Luke 10, 19. 'Behold, I have given you authority to tread on serpents and scorpions and over all the power of the enemy, and nothing will injure you.' "

On top of being used to kill the greatest believers of the Christians these last verses are also used the make Jesus a liar, because these are nothing but lies and you know this as much as I know. Faith moves mountains, this is true, but it is faith in the truth and it doesn't stop poison, snakes and scorpions to be dangerous.

And of course these murderers have someone to prove it and guess who he is. Of course it is no one else than their own master, who I think is the devil in person or yet his son. One way or the other, they are related.

See Acts 28, 3-5. 'When Paul had gathered a bundle of sticks and laid them on the fire, a viper came out because of the heat and fastened itself on his hand. When the natives saw the creature hanging from his hand, they began saying to one another: 'Undoubtedly this man is a murderer, and though he has been saved from the sea, justice has not allowed him to live.' However Paul shook the creature off into the fire and suffered no harm.'

The natives did figure him right. Jesus did just that too. See Matthew 23, 33. 'You serpents, you brood of vipers, how will you escape the sentence of hell?'

Take a look now at Isaiah 59, 5. 'They hatch adders, eggs and weave the spider web; he who eats of their eggs dies, and from that which is crushed a snake breaks forth.'

See also Matthew 7, 9-10. 'Or what man is there among you when his son asks for a loaf will give him a stone? Or if he asks for a fish, he will not give him a snake, will he?

To me the answer is quite clear. Mark, Luke, Paul and all the demons who came out of hell to do harm did it and still do it. It is most likely true that the demons that came out of hell to do harm can survive the bites of serpents, vipers and scorpions and also resist the poisonous liquids, but Jesus told us to beware of them.

Nowadays they have found out another way almost as efficient as the poison or venomous serpents to get rid of the strong believers, the ones who love God with all of their heart, soul and mind, the ones who love God more than their own life. The demons like to get rid of the ones who are about to enter the kingdom of heaven, which you won't hear about anywhere else than in Matthew.

Everyone of you have heard about missionaries, didn't you? Well yes, this is a very efficient way to get the believers killed, because their chances to come back alive from some of these countries are very slim. Don't tell me it is impossible in countries like Canada and the United States to find Africans to send to Africa or some Russians to Russia. How many of these missionaries died in action? Mark, Luke and Paul basically said that nothing could harm them. Mark, Luke and Paul might tell you they weren't true disciples. I think after all they were false prophets.

I don't doubt for one bit that God can save me from any troubles of this world and I'm sure too that my life was spared more than once. I was only seven once when through a tent I punched twice on the nose of a big bear and he went away. I doubt very much if I new what faith was all about back then. I was alive the next day, but it could very well have been the other way around.

Coming back to the pastor of the Seventh Day Adventist Church; I finally asked him if he had enough faith to try the satanic suggestion of those demons. I said it takes a lot of faith and not much common sense. Besides, if this was the case or the truth, no one could have killed Jesus or his disciples nor his apostles, nothing and no one could have hurt them.

CHAPTER 3

Many people asked me where and when I took all this information to be able to talk about it this way. Well, to tell you the truth, I didn't find it all by myself. Some people will believe me and others won't, but I do know that God speaks to me through dreams and visions. One of these dreams was quite troubling and I was tormented for most of the next day. The voice in that dream was very clear and left me with no doubt in my mind at all when it comes to its origin, because Jesus already told me that we cannot serve two masters. This voice told me that night that when I will open the Bible the next day, I will know the identity of the antichrist and this will be very obvious to me. Well, believe it or not, this is exactly what happened. I even discover the name of the beast since. Its number is six, six, six.

This happened a few months before I finished my first book called: The Precious Princess of Wonderland. This first book was given to me through a dream too, where Jesus told me that I will do it. After this second dream from the same source, I walked and I wandered all of that day, mentioning my dream to my son and to my employee, who were saying that this was only a dream. I'm usually not scared very easily by nature, but I have to admit I was shaking for most of that day. I finally armed myself with all the courage I needed at around four o'clock in the afternoon and I went to open the Bible as I was told in this dream and this the same way I was told to do it. I was already reading the Bible on a daily routine for more than thirty-eight years. Some people will say this is what drove me crazy. A priest told my grand-father years ago not to let the children read in the Bible, that this could very well trouble them. Troubled pretty well means crazy, isn't it?

The very first thing that hit me then was the fact more than two third of the New Testament was written by someone else than Jesus' apostles. Now knowing Jesus came and spent approximately three years to teach his disciples before his death and the only one who really inspires me as an apostle in the Bible is Matthew; then I asked myself this next question. What happened with the writings of all the others? I believe that the devil and the Romans will have to answer this one.

Because Jesus told us, so I know that the devil is a liar and the father of lies; I started looking for lies and contradictions in the Bible, but before doing so, I prayed and I asked God to forgive me if I was wrong for doing this. Then I told myself that if I find ten lies and contradictions or less I will forget about the whole thing. Yes I found some and this more than five hundred, 500.

This book of mine about my study is the undisputed answer, but it will be disputed by thousands of blind people, if not by millions or billions.

The second thing I found when I opened my Bible haphazardly that day is one incident or the action of a supposedly apostle who did something which is completely contrary to Jesus' teaching.

Because I know and I believe that the words in Jesus' mouth were dictated by God, the Almighty; it is him then I have to listen to, it is him I have to believe. We can read in Matthew 18, 15: 'If your brother sins, go and show him his fault in private.'

This certainly doesn't mean in front of everybody.

Take a look now, if you will in Galatians 2, 11-14. 'But when Cephas (Peter) came to Antioch, I (Paul) <u>opposed him to his face</u>, because he stood <u>condemned</u>. For prier to the coming of certain men from James, (Jesus' brother) he (Peter) used to eat with the Gentiles; but when they came, he began to withdraw and hold himself aloof, fearing the party of circumcision. The rest of the Jews joined him in his <u>hypocrisy</u>, with the result that even Barnabas was carried away by their hypocrisy. But when I saw that they were not straightforward about the truth of the gospel, <u>I (Paul) said to Cephas (Peter) in the presence of them all</u>, 'If you, being a Jew, live like the Gentiles and not like the Jews, how is it that you compel the Gentiles to live like Jews?'

Now, my friends, these from Paul were not the actions, nor the words of a Jesus' disciple or a Jesus' apostle. Paul said to Peter right in his face and this in front of everybody that he was a hypocrite.

But do you see, now that Jesus is gone to meet with his Father after his work well done, who do you think the devil should be attacking if not the most considerate of all the apostles?

See that I underlined above where Paul said: opposed him to his face. Now to oppose someone is the same thing than to resist someone. See what Jesus told us to do in such situation in Matthew 5, 39. 'But I tell you, do not resist an evil person.'

This is what Peter was to Paul for him to say that Peter stood condemned.

If Paul learned anything from Jesus or if he was with Jesus or if he followed Jesus in any way, he would have said something true at least once.

We will recognize the tree by its fruits, Jesus said. Paul with his own actions and his own words proved to me he was not my brother and neither Peter's brother, which means he is not Jesus' brother either. From then on I found hundreds of messages from Paul that contradict Jesus and God. Jesus who told me that Satan is the father of lies also showed me who the liar is.

What was wrong in Peter action? I thought of recreating the scene with today's people to better understand what went on.

Here I am sitting down with a bunch of friends at the same table where not a single chair is empty in an assembly in the West when my mom accompany by my daughter I didn't see for months suddenly walked in the hall. I excused myself quickly to my friends and I rush to the door to meet my family and I invite them to sit down at another table, because I missed them for one thing and I am very curious to know how was their trip and all the rest. Does this make me a hypocrite?

Frankly, Paul's story doesn't make any sense. Although, just like I asked, who the devil should be attacking if the master is out of the way?

After this revelation, which is out of the ordinary, I started looking for more lies and contradictions in the Bible. During a very intensive period of thirteen and a half months, more than five thousand hours reading, searching and writhing, I found five hundred and three. Most of the contradictions are about the law of God or the commandments. The law from what Jesus said not the least letter or a stroke of a pen will disappear for as long as the earth and the heaven will exist. See Matthew 5, 17-18.

This huge study led to such an enormous book so heavy in declarations about the contradictions that I think very few people can actually take it without getting troubled. I just cannot forget that one priest told my grand-father one day not to let the children read the Bible; he said that could drive them crazy. There are enough contradictions in it to drive anybody crazy, that's for sure, especially in the New Testament.

This is the reason why I decided to break it down and make different books with different stories like this book you're reading now; so it can be digested without making you too sick. I called this book: The True Face of The Antichrist. I suggest then that you read a few of my books before to be aware of this largest scandal of all times. Here are a few titles that will help you to accept the truth one step at the time. The Precious Princess of Wonderland, Always and Forever, Always and Forever + Ten Years Later, Why I Have To Die Like Jesus And Louis Riel, The Rough Road or The Golden Path? There are also a few more coming; The Hero of Heroes, The Wolf in The Sheep's Pen.

Knowing this book of True Face of The Antichrist was too heavy and knowing too that the truth is a medicine for the sick, meaning the ones who don't know the truth and live in the abomination, I then wrote a little booklet of about twenty pages, which is about ten per cent of the complete book and I called it: The Word of God. I gave one copy to my family doctor who told me afterwards that not too many people can take it. We all know that medicine has to be taken with a little spoon and this also with a lot of precautions.

God too had something to say about the Law if we pay very good attention at what is written. See Jeremiah 31, 36. 'If the Law departs from before me says the Lord, then the offspring of Israel also will cease from being a nation before me forever.'

Israel still exists and so is the Law of God, so beware of the ones who say that we are no longer under the Law and that we are under the grace.

Paul and the Romans were most likely sure, so convinced they were able to destroy the nation of Israel, this would explain why Paul said we weren't under the Law anymore, which is one of the biggest lie.

This is the exact reason why almost every country in this world, put aside Canada and the United States are against Israel and they are for the Palestine, a country of terrorists. They follow Paul. It is the reason also why so many countries tried to eliminate Israel from the face of the earth. Jerusalem belongs to Israel since forever and just know that whoever is against Israel is against God, so beware.

What I mean by contradictions is that God said one thing and someone else says the contrary or Jesus said one thing and someone else (devilish) says the contrary or the opposite. Let me give you an example of this. God said it was not good for a man to be alone and he made a woman for Adam called Eve. You know the story. Genesis 2, 18-24. Although, what is completely contrary to what God said is written by Paul in 1 Corinthians 7, 1. 'It is good for a man not to touch a woman.'

Then the brotherhood, the largest homosexual club in the world was created. The brothers and nuns, the single priest and all that hierarchy of bishops, archbishops, cardinals, popes and the abuse of thousands of young children was started also. You probably have guessed that this was originated by Paul, who some people dared called him a saint.

You must know by now too that it is very difficult to do the will of God; which is to reproduce and to fill up the earth without touching a woman. You should know by now too that whoever contradicts God comes from evil. It is not giving to everyone to sort all this out, but it is up to everyone to accept or to refuse the truth. You who are reading in this book now, I hope you realize what a chance you have to be informed, so don't waste it, because it might never come back again for you.

Jesus, who is the word of God, asked us to make disciples out of all nations, but he never said to do it twice. Besides, he said that if someone was not listening to what we have to say, to get out of there, which means to talk to the ones who want to listen.

Paul said in Romans 7, 6. 'But now we have been released from the Law, having to that by which we were bound, so that we serve in newness of the Spirit and not in oldness of the letter.'

The Law, which will never be too old, because in the kingdom of God, which is at the end of all ages and even after the thousand years of the word of God's reign, the Law will still be in the heart of the children of God, who will be happy forever after. This world, which we are living in, the world that God loved so much, according to John 3, 16 has mistreated God's own beloved son, crucified him and has never stop to persecute the people of Israel, the people of God to this day.

What is following is one of the most comforting messages to me coming from God. See Jeremiah 31, 31-34. 'Behold, days are coming, declares the Lord when I will make a new covenant with the house of Israel and with the house of Judah, not like the covenant which I made with their fathers in the day I took them by the hand to bring them out of Egypt. My covenant which they broke, although I was a husband to them, declares the Lord. But this is the covenant which I will make with the house of Israel after those days, declares the Lord. I will put my Law within them and on their heart I will write it; and I will be their God and they shall be my people.

They will not teach again each man his neighbour and each man his brother, saying know the Lord, for they will know Me, from the least of them to the greatest of them, declares the Lord, for I will forgive their iniquity and their sin I will remember no more.'

Now you can see and this according to God that his Law will never be to old for his children, but this day is not here yet even if it is not this far away, because we still have to teach our neighbour about the Law, as you can see for yourselves. Paul and the devil can say all they want, thousands of times and thousands of different ways that the Law was abolished, that it is too old and that it has passed away, the fact remains that the Law will never be out of God's children. The People of Israel still exist and so is the earth and heavens, which can still be seen and that like Jesus said, not the least stoke of a pen will disappear from it.

Although everyone with enough common sense will admit that there is a liar in there in the Bible and this is not Jesus and neither God.

Who was persecuting Jesus' disciples to death even to the foreign cities? He said it himself. See Acts 22, 4. 'I (Paul) persecuted the followers of this Way to their death, binding and putting both men and women in prisons,'

See also Acts 26, 9-11. 'So then, I thought to myself that I had to do many things hostile to the name of Jesus of Nazareth and this is just what I did in Jerusalem; not only did I lock up many of the saints in prisons, having received authority from the chief priests, but also when they were put to death, I cast my vote against them. And as I punished them often in all the synagogues, I tried to force them to blaspheme; and being furiously enraged at them, I kept pursuing them even in foreign cities.'

Now my friends, when we pay attention at what we read, we can find out that Paul wasn't saying those things to apologize or to ask for forgiveness, but to save his butts from being killed by the Jews. You see, nothing could have pleased the enemies of Jesus more than hearing these declarations. He is craftier than any the enemy. This is what Paul did all the way to Rome before all the kings and lords and all the way to Caesar. You will find the proof of this in all of Paul's travels and especially in Acts 23, 9. 'And there occurred a great uproar and some of the scribes of the pharisaic party stood up and began to argue heatedly, saying: We find nothing wrong with man.'

Paul just said he killed Jesus' disciples; there is nothing wrong with this, is there? At least this was nothing to bother Paul's conscience.

It was and it is still Rome against Israel. Paul and Rome are guilty of a lot of murders, but did they repent? Not in my book! Take a look for yourselves about Paul's declaration, See 1 Corinthians 4, 3-4. 'But to me it is very small thing that I may be examined by you or by any human court; in fact, I don't even examine myself, for I am conscious of nothing against myself.'

See now Acts 25, 8. 'While Paul said in his own defence, 'I have committed no offence either against the Law of the Jews or against the temple or against Caesar.'

I personally think that the law of the Jews also says; 'You shall not kill.'

See now what James, Jesus' brother said to Paul. Acts 21, 21. 'And they have been told about you (Paul) that you are teaching all the Jews among the Gentiles to forsake Moses, telling them not to circumcise their children nor to walk according to our customs.'

See now what Jesus had to say about Moses and the law of the Jews. See Matthew 23, 1-3. 'Then Jesus spoke to the crowds and to his disciples saying: 'The scribes and the Pharisees have seated themselves in the chair of Moses; therefore all they tell you, do and observe, but do not do according to their deeds; for they say things and they do not do them.'

The priests and the Catholic Church tell you to make children, but they don't touch that, at least in appearance.

But now we have the formal proof that Paul was teaching against the Law of God, the Law, which Jesus said that not the least stroke of a pen will disappear and against the circumcision, which is an everlasting covenant between God and his children. You can see now also that I'm not the first to blow the whistle on Paul. I owe lots of thanks to James, Jesus' brother!

Of course, if there are no Laws, there are no crimes and there are no sins either, but my God says the Law will never disappear, so it is much better to listen to and fear the One Who is able to destroy both soul and body in hell. See Matthew 10, 28.

It is a sure thing that the devil would like to see no Law in his way and be free to sin as he likes to, but you should know now what is best for you.

It is though a supposedly apostle, supposedly sent by Jesus who contradicts God and Jesus and there were billions of people who followed him and billions who are still following him. What most of them don't seem to know though is they will all be taken away with Paul, like he said it himself with his lord in the skies, on clouds, see 1 Thessalonians 4, 16-17 and be thrown in the fire like Jesus said it. See Matthew 13, 42.

I have been reading the Bible for more than fifty years now and I made a study of this one like no one I know, but today for the very first time I understood what the two will become one flesh really means. See Matthew 19, 5. 'For this reason a man will leave his father and mother and be united to his wife and the two will become one flesh.'

I have to say too that no one ever mentioned this to my ears either. I don't really know if I found about this in my dreams or in a vision, but I woke up with the answer today and this even if I never wondered about it. This is something else anyway. What do we get normally when a man gets together with a woman? The answer is a child, one flesh, one out of the two. This means indisputably that within us there are our mother and our father, even if sometimes we would like things differently.

I always said I inherited the best from them both. I am a musician like my father and honest like my mother. I am patient like my father and I am lenient like my mother. I am intelligent like my father and I am a hard worker like my mom. I am charmer like my father and I am a singer like my mom and if I don't stop this here now; I will be a bragger like my father and proud like my mom.

Although I think my dad loved God in his own way and I know my mom love God with all of her heart and because I received this gift from both of them; this would explain why I love my God with all of my heart, with all of my soul and with all of my thoughts. I also think both of them loved and had a certain talent for composition and this would explain why I composed more than two hundred and sixty songs in French and more than eighty in English. I love them all, but particularly this last one I made for my God and I called it;

You Told Me Lord
You told me oh my Lord; You brought to us the sword,
The kingdom of heaven belongs to your children.
You made beautiful things, for You I'll be pleading.
I found You amazing and for You I will sing.

You are the Father of the heavens and the earth.
You know all the secrets of the earth and the see.

Some want to take over what you created first.
Only You knows how to control the universe.

Only You can change our heart and our thoughts.
What can I do for You? For You I love so much.
From your word came my faith, now I do know my fate.
For You I want to sing, the Master of all things.

You are the Father of the heavens and the earth.
You know all the secrets of the earth and the see.
Some want to take over what you created first.
Only You knows how to control the universe.

You showed me oh my Lord that life is not a game.
Many mock you my Lord, everywhere is the shame.
Everything goes down hill, enough to make me ill.
Sing is my destiny for the eternity.

You are the Father of the heavens and the earth.
You know all the secrets of the earth and the see.
Some want to take over what you created first.
Only You knows how to control the universe.
Only You knows how to control the universe.

It is very amazing how love for God, for others and the love of a man for a woman can be inspiring.

That God made us to his image means He made us creators, because He wants us to multiply and fill up the earth to his liking. It is a sure thing that this can only happen with Adam and Eve and the ones like them, not with Adam and Steve.

CHAPTER 4

I called this chapter; it depends on which side you are.

Everything started when I was on holiday visiting my family in Quebec and we were gathering to celebrate my mom ninetieth birthday. I was in fact at her place one afternoon when a small group of her friends and acquaintances from the small church or I should say, the small assembly gets together every Sunday morning.

After a bit of discussion one of them said I should join them one of these days to understand how things are with them and that their assembly was surely different from all the Christian assemblies I have known. I said then I might just go, but this would be only if I have a chance to speak to the congregation.

So one of the people present told me then that she would have to talk to her Pastor first and get his approval to find out if I could. The only fact she called the leader of her group 'Pastor' which is the same thing than 'Father' in that sense was telling me they weren't this much different than the other Christian churches after all.

See Matthew 23, 9. 'And do not call anyone on earth 'father,' for you have one Father and He is in heaven.

You can bet the religions will make this verse disappear too one of these days.

There was only one Sunday left from the last week of my vacation and I had only two days to prepare a kind of what I will talk about if I ever was to be invited even though I was opposing just about everything they were saying. You have to understand here that when I say I oppose, it means everything and anything that opposes the word of God, which means everything that opposes the teaching of Jesus.

So I heard on the Saturday night that the Pastor gave away to their pressure and he consented to leave me talk to the assembly the next day and I wasn't yet prepared neither physically or mentally.

It is then I remembered one important message from Jesus that we can read in Matthew 10, 19-20. 'Do not worry about what to say or how to say it. At the time you will be given what to say, for it will not be you speaking, but the Spirit of your Father speaking through you.'

So I quitted worrying immediately. Like we often say; 'May God be with me.'

I could sense that my mom was worrying a lot about what will happen, she who knows my views on a lot of subjects, especially about religions. She was also afraid to lose a few friends because of it. We all know what religions do in this could also cause divisions. Louis Riel said it long before me when he said to the Judge at his trial, that Rome was the main reason for divisions in the world. There are more than twenty-five hundred Christian denominations in North America only and this directly caused by the divisions in churches. The churches ironically multiplied by the divisions within themselves.

Although my mom too, if she wants to be on Jesus' side has to carry her little cross, no matter how painful it is. This is what is necessary to be a Jesus' disciple. See Matthew 10, 38. 'And anyone who does not take his (or her) cross and follow me (the word of God) is not worthy of me.' Which means is not worthy of the word of God.

To me this is very clear, to be worthy of the word of God; we need the courage to carry our cross. We need the courage to tell others what we know about the truth and this even if we risk some frictions within friends and relatives. See what Jesus said in Matthew 10, 32. 'Whoever acknowledges me (the word of God) before men, I will also acknowledge him before my Father in heaven.'

This means I have the best lawyer of all who will intercede for me before the Great Judge.

The next verse is also very meaningful. See Matthew 10, 33. 'But whoever disowns me before men, I will disown him before my Father in heaven.'

The next few verses are very meaningful too. There is another written message that should make you reflect about the truth and you can find it in Romans 1, 18. 'The wrath of God is being revealed from heaven against all the godlessness and wickedness of men (women) who suppress the truth by wickedness.'

I could add; by their cowardice.

This is a message that gives me seal for what I'm doing, meaning exposing the liars, the lies and also tells me that I wouldn't like to be in the shoes of the ones who hid the truth, like the preachers of these Christian religions and others who did it and still do the same thing.

So, the next day, the famous Sunday I was at their little assembly of about thirty people who was expecting me with a smile on their faces. They welcomed me with joy and giving me a warm hand and they quickly introduced me to their Pastor, who seemed to be quite worried about me and didn't know too much how to hide it. He asked me to follow him a bit aside from the others and he asked me what I was intended to talk about. I had no trouble at all to understand his concerns. So I quickly tried to reassure him by telling him that I had nothing else in mind than the word of God, but for a reason I don't know and though I have a strong suspicion, this seemed to make him even more worried. So I told him not to worry, this can only be beneficial to him and to the others.

He nevertheless came up on the little stage they made up with different pieces of plywood and he announced to his congregation that this Sunday one invited guess will preach and he invited me to start as soon as I was ready.

Then he sat himself very close to me as if I needed a bodyguard. I would have preferred if he sat with all of the others, as if he considered himself equal to any member of his congregation and this way having a real conversation face to face. This would have showed me in a way he runs his church differently than the other churches' leaders as I was told a few days earlier.

I started by telling them I was going to preach differently than any other preacher they might have met in their life, that we just going to have a good discussion between us; where we will have questions and answers from both sides, a bit like Jesus was doing with his disciples when they asked him to explain the parable of the weeds. See Matthew 13, 36.

As I was saying these things I couldn't help noticing the man sitting on a chair on my right was not at ease at all, because he kept crossing his legs from right to left and then left to right. But then I have to say I was more worried about the people in front of me and their salvation, what was going to happen to them before the Great Judge than the agitated man on my right. So I asked them this very important question. 'What did you people come here for this morning? What are you looking for?'

There were at least a dozen of them who wanted to answer at the same time.

'One at the time please, otherwise I don't hear anything at all.

Let's start with this man right here in front of me and I want to hear everyone of you. Go ahead sir, tell me." "I am here because it is the day of the Lord and I like to hear the word of God." "These are some very good reasons sir, thank you."

"Your turn now. Why are you here on this particular morning?" "It is for me the same reasons, but I will add that it is also because I like the reunion between my friends and because we are a small group, this is even more pleasant to me." "I see and I understand very well your point of view."

"And what about you, what is your reason? You're not very young anymore as I can see." "No, I'm getting to be pretty old and I can tell you that I have been around just about all the churches, but it is here that I feel the best." "But what did you learn in all those years? How old are you?" "I am eighty-two years and a few months old." "How long have you been going to church?" "My parents were taking me to church since I was four." "But what did you learn in seventy-eight years?" "Well, I learned that we have to go to church every Sunday; that we have to confess our sins and love our neighbour." "I think you shouldn't have any business over here at all anymore. You should have learned enough by now and this for a very long time to teach others instead of coming here or anywhere else, because if you don't know God and his will after all of these years, I have a hard time believing you might know Him some day. Although today might just be the day you will understand."

"What about you, my nice lady? What did you come to get here this morning?" "I love so much the voice of our dear Pastor and the way he talks to us about Paul; the so great apostle and his achievements and all his sufferings he's been through, the poor man. I also love all the hymns that we sing to the Lord." "But do you hear about Jesus and all of the other apostles and disciples who were following Jesus everywhere?" "Which apostles are you talking about sir?" "I will come back to it a bit later Mrs., if you allow me of course."

"And you young girl, what are you looking for in an assembly like this one?" "Me, I just try to understand, but I must admit; it doesn't seem to happen very quickly. I was told this will come some day." "You can always take example on the older people who are still looking after seventy-eight years. Do you read the Bible some time?" "No, I find it too complicated." "So for what I can see; you are putting your destiny or the destiny of your soul in the hands of someone else? You blindly put your trust in others?" "I thing this might just be the case sir."

"And you young man, would you have a different reason than any of the others?" "Me, of course I have a different reason. If I don't come to church every Sunday morning, my mom wouldn't be happy with me at all." "It is a reason and it is just as good as any others, because it is written; 'Honour your mom and dad.'"

"Anyone else would like to tell me why he comes to church every Sunday morning?" "Well, if I wasn't here I doubt very much there would be a service that day." "And what do you think of this morning service?" "No one will be able to say it is not different, this is for sure." "Can you tell me why you chose to sit apart from everyone else?" "I don't think there is a particular reason; it just happened this way." "You are reassuring me, because I thought it was maybe to jump me if I made a bad move."

There was some laugh, but mostly a forced laugh from most of them. I took a deep breath and I said:

"So, if I understand right, most of you people are here today because it is the day of the Lord?"

Most of them made an affirmation sign with their head.

"Does any of you ever read the Bible or all of you are trusting your church leaders this blindly?"

The man on my right straightened himself up right away on his chair, but he didn't dare saying anything.

"Is there someone who could read out loud Exodus 20, from verses eight to eleven, please?"

There were many hands up, but I had nevertheless to make a choice among them.

You there on the second row, read out loud if you can." "Remember the Sabbath day by keeping it holy. Six days you shall labour and do all your work, but the seventh day is a Sabbath to the Lord your God. On it you shall not do any work, neither you, nor your son or daughter, nor your manservant or maid-servant, nor your animals, nor the alien within your gates. For in seven days the Lord made heavens and the earth, the sea and all that is in them, but He rested on the seventh day. Therefore the Lord blessed the Sabbath day and made it holy.'"

"Thank you very much Mrs, you've done a very good job. Now I noticed when I came in earlier there was a young child among you and I would like to ask him if he could show us on a calendar where are the first and the last day of the week." "This is our little James who is four years old." "Could he come up here with his mother and a calendar please?" "Of course he can, we are coming right away sir."

"Hi James. Do you know that I have the same first name? You are a big boy, how old are you?" "Me, I am four years old." "Do you know how to count?" "Of course I know. One, two, three, four, five, six, ten." "This is very good; you will go a long way in life. See this calendar; there are a lot of numbers on it. Can you tell me where is the first number on this line?" "Yes, this is the first and this is the last one." "Congratulation my boy, you might just have opened the eyes of many people today and thank you very much for your incalculable help."

"What if I ask now the mother of this child to show us where James said the last day of the week was and what its name is?" "James told us that Saturday is the seventh day, so the last day of the week and that Sunday is the first." "Somebody said one day: 'The truth comes out of the mouth of a child.'

Yes, the truth comes out of the mouth of children and from those as these just like the kingdom of heaven. Thank you very much Mrs. for your help also. Just know that I appreciate it a lot."

It was then a complete silence in the house and I started to understand that each and everyone in there were paying a particular attention to all of my words.

"Now, if I understand well, I believe all of you made an enormous mistake by coming here today." "We didn't make mistakes at all; I would rather say that we were lied to." "You cannot blame everyone else; the Bible is there for everybody. If a young child of four years old can read a calendar; this means that everyone of you can read the Bible and pay attention to what you're reading. There is a very good reason why Jesus said: 'Seek and you will find.'

He also said to be careful when we read and there was a very good reason for that too. See Matthew 24, 15."

"But why were we always told that the Sunday is the day of the Lord, the day to serve Him?" "Can't you see that we were lied to? So we have to find out who is guilty of this enormous sin. When you'll know who he is; you'll know who the antichrist is too." "Why wouldn't you tell us who he is?" "I need to make sure first that none of you brought some stones in this assembly. This could shock some of you and I would like to get out of here alive. I suggest then that we cast a vote on this question. Can the ones who want to know lift up your hand please? I can see this is the majority, but by a small margin.

I would like first that someone reads Matthew 5, 17-18. I want to make sure everyone understands that absolutely nothing was changed from the law since Jesus talked about it. Who wants to volunteer for this reading? One thing is sure; there are a lot of volunteers over here. You there from the last row, read out loud please."

"'Do not think that I have come to abolish the Law or the Prophets; I have not come to abolish them but to fulfill them. I tell you the truth, <u>until heaven and earth disappear</u>, not the smallest letter, not the least stroke of a pen; will by any means disappear from the Law until everything is accomplished.'"

"So, all of you can understand very well that absolutely nothing was or is changed from the Law of God and this directly from the mouth of Jesus, one of the greatest Prophet and this also from another great Prophet and this is Moses. See Deuteronomy 18, 18.

None of you is too blind to see that heaven and earth still exist and still can be seen. So let's look for the guilty party, would you? Is there someone who would like to read Acts, 20, 7, please?" "'<u>On the first day of the week</u> we came together to break bread. <u>Paul</u> spoke to the people and, because he intended to leave the next day, kept on talking until midnight.'"

"Thanks a lot sir, I always appreciate the ones who can read in public. Don't you worry, I won't keep you up until midnight for fear you fall asleep and fall down from your chair; which would be a lot less dangerous than falling from the third floor like one of Paul's disciples.

There is another reference about the first day of the week as I can remember and this one is in 1 Corinthians 16, 2. May I have another volunteer to read it please? No one dares? Do you want to read again sir? Go ahead, we are listening to you." "'<u>On the first day of every week</u>, each one of you should set aside a sum of money in keeping with his income, saving it up, so that when I (Paul) come no collection will have to be made.'"

"Paul had to be on his way as soon as possible and I doubt very much that any of this money went to Jerusalem, not more than it does today. Although, you all know now where, when and who started the story of the first day of the week, which is opposing the Law of God given to Moses and confirmed by Jesus.

In case any of you doesn't know it; there were many people in the ancient time that had the sun for their god. All of you who are here today, why are you keeping the first day of the week, Sunday, the day of the sun, instead of following the Law of God by sanctifying the resting day of the true God, the Sabbath, the seventh day of the week as God asked us to do? Can anyone answer this question or is it too embarrassing?"

I couldn't help noticing that all the eyes were turning towards their Pastor for an answer. Nevertheless, neither him dared answer this question. He too seemed to be embarrassed by this last one.

The answer is very simple my friends. It is because you have been following Paul instead of following Jesus and you heard about Paul a lot more than you heard about Jesus. Who is to blame? Well, it is not mine to judge you, but it is up to everyone of you to examine your conscience and to see for yourselves if you are responsible for your own ignorance. Didn't you look for the truth or did you look where there was no truth? I know though it is never too late to do the right thing.

From now on you will have no more excuse for not looking for the truth and you cannot count only on everybody else to do it for you. You've done that and you can see where this led you. Let me tell you too that you have an extraordinary luck today that someone is opening your eyes about the liar and it is not everybody who has this luck."

"Can you tell us how come you know all these things that our priests and our pastors never talked about?" "Well.....you see for me, I have no religion to protect and I have no reason at all to hide the truth, on the contrary; I have every reason in the world to spread the truth, to make it known to everybody." "But this doesn't explain why you seem to know all these things that all of us ignore." "Well, I follow the true God and I follow his servant Jesus, who told us to be careful when we read. It is written in Matthew 24, 15. 'So when you see standing in the holy place, (in the Bible) the abomination that causes desolation,' spoken of through the prophet Daniel,—let the reader understand.'

So, this is it, I saw the abomination that causes me desolation standing in the holy place, in the Bible and I have been careful to what I was reading. Me, Jesus and God are one." "But you're not going to tell us that you are God or Jesus, are you?" "I wouldn't never dare saying such a thing," "But this is what you just said." "I did this, no way." "We all heard you clearly." "I think you misunderstood me. What did I say exactly?" "You said you were God and Jesus." "No, I'm sorry, but this is not what I said and it is impossible I could have said this."

"You sir, on my right and who are very close to me, did you hear the same thing? Is there anyone who can repeat the exact same words I said?" "We can do better than this. Everything is recorded; we only have to roll the video back. Here we are. 'Me, Jesus and God are one.'"

"So I see, you misunderstood me. Would you roll it back a bit farther, please and hear what I said?" "Sure!" 'Well, I follow the true God and I follow his servant Jesus.'

Yes I follow God and Jesus, but you, who are you following? No one dare to answer this. I'm going to tell you who you are following, especially by coming here on Sunday morning. You have followed and you are following men who teach Paul, the liar and this is why you ignore the truth.

I would like someone to read John 17, 21." "'That all of them (Jesus' disciples) may be one, Father, just as You are in me and I am in You. May they also be in us so that the world may believe that You sent me.'"

"Now, if Jesus prayed God for his disciples to be one with him and with God, the Father, why it is so incredible for me to say I am one with Jesus and with God?"

From then on I was expecting the man on my right to get up abruptly and say this was enough, but he didn't do anything; mainly I think for fear to be disapproved by the rest of the assembly.

"Do you remember reading Matthew 15, 14? 'Leave them; they are blind guides. If a blind man leads a blind man, both will fall into a pit.'

If a person ignores the truth teaches another person who ignores the truth, what will he learn? Chances would be very good they only learn the lies."

And one more time, all the eyes in the room were looking at the man on my right; who was not at ease at all on his chair. I think he would have preferred and by far not to participate to such a meeting. But on the other hand, if he decided to go away, he would have been judged by his congregation as someone who was not interested in the truth, just like many pastors and priests I have known by the way.

"Are you telling us that all the priests and pastors don't know the truth?" "Very far away from me is that thought. If this was the case, many pastors I have known wouldn't have told members of their congregation to avoid me and mainly not to talk to me. It is a sure thing that the truth will empty the churches and for most of the teachers making a living this way is more important than the truth. It is a sure thing too that the pastor who told my sister who mentioned a few things I talked about not to show up at his church anymore knows the truth, but he doesn't want this truth to be spread out to his people. The pastor who told his congregation at the church where I used to go not to talk to me anymore knows the truth and he is afraid of it. I didn't give him a chance to throw me out the door, I was ahead of him.

But if you agree with me now; I would like to talk to you about the key of all the humanity, the key of all the schemes. You will understand that contrary to many teachers, I teach and I preach Jesus. Is there someone who can tell me which key I am talking about?" "Are you talking about the key of the kingdom of heaven that was given to Peter from Jesus, something I never really understood?" "Yes and no, I mean not precisely. I'm talking here about the most important message from Jesus to us concerning the humanity. The key you're talking about and was given to Peter is simply the truth, the word of God and when we receive it and live by it, this key opens to us the doors of the kingdom of heaven that Jesus talked so often about in Matthew and that no other evangelist even mentioned the word. You can look all you want anywhere else than in Matthew; you will not find these words: The kingdom of heaven. But if you don't mind I'll come back to this later on.

People who follow the truth don't go to church anymore, which displease enormously their leaders. The more than five thousand men who were following Jesus (the truth, the word of God) everywhere weren't going to the synagogues (churches) anymore and this was frustrating the Pharisees enough to give them the desire to kill him.

Jesus is the word of God; he is the truth and the truth is emptying the churches and this is why most of the pastors and priests don't want it. It is understandable too, because people in their churches are bread on their table. It is very sad, but this is the way it is.

Here I want to talk to you about the parable of the weeds and its explanation from Jesus.

Then Jesus told them (his disciples) who planted the good seed, the word of God, the truth and this was himself, the Son of Man, the true Prophet. He told them the field was the world; the good seed was also the sons of the kingdom, (his followers) He told them also the weeds were the son of the devil, the liars. You understand all this up to now?" "This would mean that Jesus spread the truth in the world and the devil spread something too, but he spread the lies. That's what it is, isn't it?" "There is only one thing missing in your statement, do you know what it is? No one can answer this? The two, meaning the truth Prophet and the false prophet made their work at the same time, which means in the same garden. The devil was already personified at the time of Jesus. John, Jesus' brother said it and you can read this in 1 John 4, 2-3. Can I get someone to read this please?" "You said 1 John....?" "1 John 4, 2-3." "'This is how you can recognize the Spirit of God: Every spirit that acknowledges that Jesus Christ has come in the flesh is from God, but every spirit that does not acknowledge Jesus is not from God. This is the spirit of the antichrist, which you have heard is coming and even now is already in the world.'"

"Thank you Mrs. I appreciate this a lot.

Now, whoever is still awaiting the coming of the antichrist is certainly misinformed, because the antichrist was already in the world at the time of Jesus and his disciples. I can assure you that I am here today to confess Jesus and to make his messages known to you.

Let's get back to the parable of the weeds now. What is following almost says it all. See Matthew 13, 39. 'And the enemy who sows them (the lies, present time) is the devil.'

Now, to be able to find who the enemy of Jesus is, who is the enemy of the truth, the enemy of the Law of God and who is also opposing the teaching of Jesus, you only have to listen to Jesus who said in Matthew 24, 15. 'Be careful when you read.'

'The harvest is the end of the world, (meaning the end of the kingdom of the devil) the harvesters are God's angels.' The ones who serve God continuously.

'The Son of Man (Jesus, the word of God) will send out his angels and they will weed out of his kingdom everything that causes sin and all who do evil. (This will be on earth) The angels then will throw them into the fiery furnace, (which is out of the kingdom of heaven) where there will be weeping and gnashing of teeth. (Which cannot happen in a temperature of more than two thousand degrees or more.) Then the righteous will shine like the sun in the kingdom of their Father. He who has ears, let him hear.'

Which means, may the ones who have understanding understand all this.

The only fact the evil ones won't be able to hurt the righteous anymore will be enough the make them gnashing their teeth and give them burning, which will be a lot worst than heartburn. And this will be also enough to give the righteous a paradise on earth to the ones left, because there will be no one to persecute them anymore. What do you think of all this?" "I think it is a question of interpretation." "I agree with you on this question, although, even though there are many explanations or interpretations, there is only one truth, the truth.

Is there anyone among you people who thinks that Jesus is a liar?"

All of them shook their head negatively.

"So this means if Jesus is telling the truth, this also means the ones who say the opposite, the contrary are lying and they are liars. We already saw that Paul said contrary to Jesus concerning the Law of God, but I would like to go a bit farther and show you other points about this supposedly apostle." "It seems too that you have quite a grudge against Paul. I'm I mistaking or not?" "I would tell you; yes and no. It is not mine to judge anyone, although, it is up to me and it is up to every Jesus' disciple to expose the lies and the liars. It is one thing to lie about the time one went to bed last night; I don't say it is right and the consequences are more or less so, so, but it is a different thing to lie about the word of God. When we pay attention to what Jesus said; it is then possible to know who said the opposite of what he said or the opposite of his messages. This is what I'm trying to make you see, to make you understand. If you allow me now, we'll go see together some of these lies and contradictions.

CHAPTER 5

Paul Lied and condemned

Let's see first the beginning of his ministry, starting with his supposed conversion in Acts 9, 7. 'The men travelling with Saul (Paul) stood there speechless; they <u>heard</u> the sound but did <u>not see</u> anyone.'

See now Acts 9, 9. 'For three days he (Paul) was blind and did not eat or drink anything.'

Paul was blind according to him by Jesus. But we should all know that Jesus is opening the eyes of the blind, he doesn't close them.

Acts 9, 10. 'In Damascus there was a <u>disciple</u> named Ananias.'

Let's go see now what happening with Paul in Acts 22, 9. 'My companions <u>saw</u> the light, but they <u>did not hear</u> the voice of him who was speaking to me.'

So, either they heard or they didn't hear the voice of the one who was speaking and either they saw or didn't see the light.

See now what it is written in Acts 9, 19. 'Saul (Paul) spent several days with the disciples in Damascus.'

See now Paul in Galatians 1, 16. 'I did not consult any man.'

Do I have to remind you that Jesus was a man, for he said in Matthew 26, 26. 'This is my body.' He also said in

Matthew 26, 28. 'This is my blood.' It was also said that none of his bones will be broken. See John 19, 36.

Jesus said he doesn't condemn anyone and more; he said that he didn't even come to judge. See what Paul did in Hebrew 6, 4-6. Not only Paul judged, but he condemned everybody, including the Jesus' apostles and I strongly believe this is one of the worst abominations in the Bible. But Jesus said to his apostles they will be sitting with him on twelve thrones to judge the twelve tribes of Israel. See Matthew 19, 27.

Hebrew 6, 4-6. 'It is impossible for those who have once been enlightened, (like the apostles) who have tasted the heavenly gift, (like the Jesus' apostles) who have shared in the Holy Spirit, (like the apostles) who have tasted the goodness of the word of God and the power of the coming age, (like the apostles) if they fall away, (like all the apostles did) to be brought back to repentance, because, to their lost they are crucifying the son of God all over again.'

When I say the devil condemns everybody; you have quite an example of it here above.

Let me tell you that the eleven apostles left after Jesus death and also Matthias, the one who replaced Judas, the trader, all have been enlightened, they all have tasted the heavenly gift, they all have shared in the Holy Spirit, they all have tasted in the goodness of the word of God and in the power of the coming age and they all fell and this for the salvation of all of us. See Matthew 26, 56. 'Then all the disciples deserted him and fled.'

Yes they fell and if they didn't, they would have all most likely been killed, crucified along with Jesus. Then Jesus would have waste three years of his life, because the word of God would have been crucified with them. Can you imagine only have the gospel of Paul? See, it is the work of the devil to condemn everybody, but you, you don't have to put up with the devil and you can chase this demon out of your life. Remember what Jesus said in Matthew 24, 15. 'When you'll see the abomination that causes the desolation, may the reader be careful when he read.'

Well, let me tell you that I was careful with what I was reading and I saw the abomination in the holy place and I am desolated to see it. The Bible has been called saint for a very long time now, hasn't it?

I found more than five hundred lies and contradictions in it and this in my first study only. Just check this one out with me please in Hebrew 11, 11. 'By faith even Sarah herself received ability to conceive, even beyond the proper time of life, since she considered Him faithful who had promised.'

Maybe Sarah obeyed because she feared God just like Abraham, but for what I concluded by reading her story, she didn't believe at all and she rather laughed, especially when she heard the story of her pregnancy. See Genesis 18, 12-13. 'So Sarah laughed to herself as she thought, "After I am worn out and my master (husband) is old, will I now have this pleasure?" Then the Lord said to Abraham, "Why did Sarah laugh and say, "Will I really have a child, now that I am old."'"

"Do you really think she had faith? Do you think she believed when the Lord told her she will get pregnant? I don't.

See now Genesis 17, 17. 'Abraham fell facedown; he laughed and said to himself, "Will a son be born to a man a hundred years old? Will Sarah bear a child at the age of ninety?'

Sarah and Abraham feared God maybe and had obedience and they were righteous, but when it comes to have faith about them having a child at their old age, I have my doubts about this one.

Do you see now that Paul do and say everything that is contrary to what Jesus and his apostles said? Jesus was preaching repentance, love for God and obedience in the Law of God. Paul preached faith and against the Law. This is not all. Remember that Jesus said not to swear at all.

Paul swears

What is following is something the liars use a lot, but the Jesus' disciples don't do it, simply because Jesus told us not to. See Paul in 2 Corinthians 1, 23. 'I call God as a witness to my soul, that to spare you I did not come again to Corinth.'

I too would say they were spared if Paul didn't return there.

To see more swearing from Paul see also Romans 1, 9, 2 Corinthians 11, 31, Philippians 1, 8, 1 Timothy 5, 21, 2 Timothy 4, 1.

See what Jesus said about swearing, which is taking God as witness.

Matthew 5, 34-37. 'But I (Jesus) say to you, make no oath at all, either by heaven, for it is the throne of God, or by the earth, for it is the footstool of his feet, or by Jerusalem, for it is the city of the great King. Nor shall you make an oath by your head, for you cannot make one hair white or black. But let your statement be yes, yes, or no, no, anything beyond these is of evil.'

And one more time Jesus showed me who the devil is. No one can be clearer than this. You most likely know the real definition of swearing, don't you? If I remember well the catechist and what I learned in school from it when I was still young, it goes like this. "Swearing or making an oath is to take God as our witness to our affirmation."

To do it is antichrist. Does it begin to sink in? Jesus gave us a good message also about judging others. Let's go see what Paul did.

Paul judged

Let's see first what Jesus said on the subject. See Matthew 7, 1-2. 'Do not judge so that you will not be judged. For in the way you judge, you will be judged and by your standard of measure it will be measured to you.'

See Paul in 1 Corinthians 6, 2-3. 'Or do you not know that the saints will judge the world? If the world is judge by you, are you not competent to constitute the smallest law courts? Do you not know that we will judge the angels? How much more matters of this life?'

Not only Paul was judging others, but he was also teaching his disciples to do the same thing. Not only Paul was judging people, contrary to the will of God, but he didn't waste any time before judging the angels of heaven also.

But see, the one who is sitting in God's temple, the one who has so many children can do anything he wants, for him there is no law and there is no sin.

See now 1 Galatians 1, 8-9. 'But even if we or an angel from heaven should preach a gospel other than the one we preached to you, (which are lies and contradictions) let him be eternally condemned! As we have already said, so now I (Paul) say again, if anybody is preaching to you a gospel other than what you accepted, let him be eternally condemned.'

Not only Paul Judged people, he Judged the angels of heaven and not only he blasphemed, but he repeated his blasphemy.

This is a story though that tells me there were some people among Paul's listeners who knew the truth, the word of God, the Jesus' messages, for Paul to speak like this.

See now how he, Paul judged the others. See 1 Timothy 5, 24. 'The sins of some men are quite evident even before we judge them.'

See also Romans 3, 4. 'So you triumph when you judge.'

See Paul again in 1 Corinthians 5, 3. 'For I, on my part, though absent in body but present in <u>spirit</u>, have already <u>judged</u> him who have so committed this, as though I was present.'

There we are; the spirit who was to come is in the picture. Only in John gospel we can see the word Counselor that Jesus will send over. In other English Bible instead of Counselor I saw the words Helper and Comforter, but no where else it is mentioned than in John 14, 16, 14, 26, 15, 26, 16, 7 and 16, 13 except in Job 29, 25.

This is where Paul was introduced. See now 1 Corinthians 4, 3-4. 'But to me it is a very small thing that I may be judged by you or by any human court; in fact, I do not judge myself. For I am conscious of nothing against myself.'

The spirit has spoken, but believe it, Paul is not the Holy Spirit; he is quite the opposite. This man was arresting and killing the Jesus' disciples, but of course, if there is no law for him, there is no sin and no crime.

See 1 Corinthians 11, 31. 'But if we judge ourselves rightly, we would not be judged.'

See Acts 23, 2-3. The high priest Ananias commanded those standing beside him (Paul) to strike him on the mouth. Then Paul said to him, 'God is going to strike you whitewashed wall! Do you sit to try me according to the Law, and in violation of the Law order me to be struck?'

I think Paul was talking about the Roman's law, for it was extremely dangerous for a Jew to strike a Roman in those days. He just said it didn't matter to him to be judged by anyone or any human court. What it would have been if this was important to him? The Roman soldiers would have destroyed the court and the judge. This is most likely what happened. Paul knew there were an army of soldiers outside just waiting for a signal and they were there to protect any Roman against any Jew or any Israel court. If you look for yourselves; you too will find many verses where Paul judged others and taught to do the same even if some were arguing with him. Nevertheless, it is very easy to see here that Paul was teaching contrary to what Jesus was teaching. And what about the confession in many churches, isn't it a form of judgement?

Paul, a hypocrite

Paul's own testimony in 1 Corinthians 9, 19-22 proves his hypocrisy. 'Though I am and belong to no man, I make myself a slave to everyone, to win as many as possible. (By craftiness) To the Jews I became like a Jew, (Paul said before he is a Jew) to win the Jews. To those under the Law I became like one under the Law, though I myself am not under the law, so as to win those under the law. To those not having the law I became like one not having the law, (this should have been easy enough for him) (though I am not free from God's Law, but am under Christ's law, (this got to be the antichrist law) so as to win those not having the law. To the weak I became weak, to win the weak. I have become all things to all men so that by all possible means I might save some.' (To hand them over to Satan)

And Paul thinks himself as a saviour on top of all.

I don't see myself becoming a sinner to save another sinner and I don't think Jesus did this either. I also think it takes someone strong to help the weak, not only physically, but also spiritually.

See 1 Corinthians 10, 8. 'We should not commit sexual immorality, as some of them did—and in one day twenty-three thousand of them died.'

Maybe one thousand of them escaped the trap of the devil, because this was not twenty-three thousand who died that day but twenty-four thousand. See the true story in Numbers 25, 9. 'Then the plague against the Israelites was stopped; but those who died in the plague numbered 24, 000.'

See Acts 23, 4-5. 'But the bystanders said; 'Do you revile God's high priest?' And Paul said, 'I was not aware, brethren that he was high priest, for it is written; 'You shall not speak evil of a ruler of your people.'

The hypocrite, he was working for them.

Look at Acts 26, 10. 'And this is just what I did in Jerusalem; not only I lock up many of the saints in <u>prisons</u>, having received authority from the chief priests, but also when they were being put to death, I cast my vote against them.'

I recognized the tree by its fruits! Thanks to you Jesus.

And from here all the way to Rome Paul saved his head by telling the same story that he chased all the way to the foreign cities, that he arrested, put them in prisons and killed the Jesus' disciples.

Take a look too at Acts 26, 12. 'While so engaged as I was journeying to Damascus with the authority and commission of the chief priests.'

See Acts 22, 4-5. 'I persecuted this Way to their death, binding and putting both men and women into prisons, as also <u>the high priest and all the council of the elders can testify</u>. From them I also received letters to the brethren and started off to Damascus in order to bring even those who were there in Jerusalem as prisoners to be punished.'

Can you see that the high priests were Paul's brothers and so were the Damascus brothers. Ananias from Damascus, the so called disciple was one of them too. See Acts 9, 10-19.

In Acts 9, 20, Paul had started already to disobey Jesus. 'And immediately he began to proclaim Jesus in the <u>synagogues</u>, saying, 'He is the son of God.'

Look at Matthew 10, 1-17. Jesus told his apostles to enter some deserving houses and that we will be scourged in the synagogues. It is clear to me that Jesus wanted his disciples to stay away from the synagogues. Besides, the Jews wouldn't let Paul and no one else preaching in their synagogues in those days, especially not to say that Jesus was the son of God. See John 19, 7. 'The Jews answered him, 'We have a law and by that law he ought to die because he made himself out to be the son of God.

The Pharisees didn't allow Jesus to say he is the Son of God and they wouldn't allow Paul to say that either, at least not in their synagogues or in the temple.

Wasn't it him, Paul who accused Peter to be a hypocrite? See Galatians 2, 11-16.

Do you understand now that there was nothing in the world that could please more the Pharisees, the Sadducees, the kings and all the roman leaders all the way from Jerusalem to Rome? For them to hear that one of their own (Paul) was destroying the enemy of Rome was exceptional. He is crafty the devil and Paul too. All of this happened after the so called conversion of Paul to Jesus.

Paul made it to Rome saving his life by telling who ever wanted to hear it that he persecuted to death the Jesus' disciples and this even after his supposedly conversion to Jesus. This was quite a way to be an apostle. Telling the truth that it is on this man, this Paul and his teaching that the Christian Churches were founded makes me a target just like Jesus and Louis Riel! If you can count all the Christians or I should say all the ones who believe that the Bible is the absolute truth, then you can almost count all my enemies. Read Matthew 10, 34. 'Do not think that I came to bring peace on the earth; I did not come to bring peace, but a sword.'

Let me show you another story about Paul where there is no more hypocrisy. It is the story where and when he circumcised Timothy; him (Paul) who constantly spoke against it and whoever practiced it; meaning the circumcision group. See Galatians 5, 12. 'As for those agitators, (the circumcision group who was working hands, in hands with the Jesus' apostles) I (Paul) wish they would go the whole way and emasculate themselves.'

This is quite a wish coming from an apostle, don't you think? God's wish is quite different as we'll see in Genesis 1, 28. 'God blessed them, (people, Adam and Eve) and God said to them: Be fruitful and multiply and fill the earth and subdue it.'

This is quite different from the castration. See also Genesis 9, 1, where God repeated the same message, his will with Noah and his family this time. 'Then God blessed Noah and his sons, saying to them, "Be fruitful and increase in number and fill the earth.'

Luckily for me, my dad and many other normal men listened to God rather than listening to Paul.

Paul's wish was and is completely contrary to the wish of God that is the fill up the earth.

See now what Paul did to Timothy, the one he called, "My son." Paul who wished all men should be like he is, meaning not to touch a woman. See Acts 16, 3. 'Paul wanted this man (Timothy, the one he called his son) to go with him and he took him and he circumcised him, because of the Jews who were in those parts, for they all knew that his father was a Greek.'

If this is not hypocrisy, then tell me what it is. Him, Paul who called the group of the circumcision, "Mutilators" did the same thing and this most likely to save his life again. Now, if you look carefully for the messages where Paul talked against the circumcision and the ones who practiced it, you will find dozens of them. Keep in mind too that this same circumcision is an everlasting covenant between God and his children. If you keep looking for Paul's messages of hypocrisy, you too will find many of them.

Paul's slanders

See 1 Thessalonians 2, 2. 'We (Paul and his disciples) had previously suffered and been insulted in Philippi, as you know, but with the help of our God we dare to tell you his gospel in spite of strong opposition.'

See now what the same man, this hypocrite said to the Philippians in Philippians 1, 4-5. 'In all my prayers for all of you, I (Paul) always pray with joy because of your partnership in the gospel from the first day until now.'

Some could think his god allowed him to slander also. Here is another one from Paul. At least this was not talking well about someone. See 2 Timothy 4, 14-15. 'Alexander the metalworker did me a great deal of harm, the Lord will repay him for what he has done. You too should be on your guard against him, because he strongly opposed our message.'

Paul said many times that deeds don't count. I see that I'm not the first one to see Paul's lies and contradictions.

Jesus or one of his disciples would have said: "May God forgive him if this is possible."

This is what Peter did. See Acts 8, 22. 'Repent of this wickedness and pray to the Lord. Perhaps He will forgive you for having such thought in your heart.'

Paul condemns and he is against the circumcision, which is an everlasting covenant between God and Abraham and his whole offspring. See Genesis 17, 1-13.

Everlasting really means forever, isn't it? Hold on to your hat, because there is a lot about this one.

See Galatians 5, 2. 'Behold I, Paul say to you that if you receive circumcision, Christ will be of no benefit to you.'

The truth is that if you get circumcision, it is the false christ, the antichrist that will be of no benefit to you. Poor Timothy, the friend or the imaginary son of Paul, according to Paul himself, you are lost and Christ is no benefit to you, because your father, the one who has begotten you has also circumcised you. What a shame. It must be very sad to be condemned to hell by your one friend or your own father.

See Zechariah 11, 15-17. 'Then the Lord said to me, "Take again the equipment of a foolish shepherd. For I am going to raise up a shepherd over the land who will not care for the lost, or seek the young, or heal the injured, or feed the healthy, but will eat the meat of the choice sheep, tearing off their hoofs. "Woe to the worthless shepherd, who deserts the flock! May the sword strike his arm and his right eye! May his arm be completely withered, his right eye totally blinded!"

This, my friend, I believe is the thorn in the flesh of Paul, the thorn he mentioned himself in 2 Corinthians 12, 7.

This would also explain why the viper couldn't hurt him; Paul's right arm was dead. See Acts 28, 3-5. 'Paul gathered a pile of brushwood and, as he put it on the fire, a viper, driven out by the heat, fastened itself on his hand. When the Islanders saw the snake hanging from his hand, they said to each other, "This man must be a murderer, for though he escaped from the sea, Justice has not allowed him to live." But Paul shook the snake off his hand into the fire and suffered no ill effects.'

The Islanders figured Paul right on, for he is a murderer. The other thorn in Paul's flesh most likely was a blind right eye. See also what he said in Galatians 4, 15. 'What has happened to all your joy? I can testify that, if you could have done so, you would have torn out your eyes and given them to me.'

I personally think the Galatians did the same thing the Islanders did and I did, they figured out Paul is the devil, a liar, a murderer and the outlaw. See John 8, 44. Jesus too figured him out right.

In the supposedly Paul's writings, we can read in Romans 12, 14. 'Bless those who persecute you; bless and do not curse.'

See now what Paul did in Galatians 1, 8-9. 'But even if we or an angel from heaven should preach a gospel other than the one we preached to you, let him be eternally condemned! As we have already said, so now I (Paul) say again, if anybody is preaching to you a gospel (full of lies) other than what you accepted, let him be eternally condemned.'

Not only Paul blasphemed against an angel of heaven, but he repeated his blasphemy. It is not enough for him to condemn men and to hang them over to Satan, but he attack also the angels of heaven. Only a satanic person or Satan himself can do such a thing.

Here we have to be very careful when we read, because those words are very misleading.

See 1 Corinthians 5, 4-5. 'When you are assembled in the name of our Lord Jesus and <u>I am with you in spirit</u>, and the power of our Lord Jesus is present, hand this man over to Satan, so the sinful nature may be destroyed and his spirit saved on the day of the Lord.'

How can a person sound in body and mind believes that being handed over to Satan can be saved on the day of the Lord? I saw a lot of devilish things in the Bible, but rarely as devilish as this few lines.

This is also the formal proof that Paul tried to make the world believe he is the spirit that Jesus was to send after his departure and mainly announced by John, the Paul's disciple. Who came in the picture after Jesus' departure, if this is not Paul? Ho, he is crafty the devil and he said it himself. See Genesis 3, 1 and 2 Corinthians 12, 16. 'Be that as it may, I have not been a burden to you. Yet, crafty fellow that I am, I caught you by trickery.'

See John 14, 16, 14, 26, 15, 26, 16, 7, 16, 13 and Acts 1, 8, 2, 4, 2, 33, 2, 38, 8, 16. See also the one who sowed the weeds in Matthew 13, 36-43.

This is why I say the John of the gospel of John is not the John of Jesus, his apostle, but the John, disciple of Paul, at least, in the biggest part. John the Baptist opened the way for Jesus, the Christ, the true Prophet and the John of the gospel of John opened the way for Paul, the antichrist.

See John 7, 39. 'By this he meant the Spirit, whom those who believed in him were later to receive. Up to that time the Spirit had not been given, since Jesus had not yet been glorified.'

The Spirit of God has been in the world since it was created. See Luke 1, 67. 'His father Zechariah was filled with the Holy Spirit and prophesied.'

Zechariah was in the world long before Jesus was born. Everywhere you'll see the writhing of the prophets, you'll see also that the Spirit of God was on and with them. Let me explain another thing to you here. The author of the gospel of John tried to make people believe the Spirit of God was not yet in the world, which is false, of course. It is a sure thing too that Paul tried to make the world believe he was the one to come, him who has begotten many sons and this without touching a woman.

See again Matthew 10, 19-20. 'Do not worry about what to say or how to say it. At the time you will be given what to say, for it will not be you speaking, but the Spirit of your Father speaking through you.'

And this even if Jesus didn't returned to his Father yet.

See Paul in Colossians 2, 5. 'For though I am absent from you in body, I (Paul) am with you in spirit and delight to see how orderly you are and how firm your faith in Christ is.'

The one who sat himself in God's temple, Paul sees everything. See 2 Thessalonians 2, 4.

This is my explanation as to know that this John, Paul's John is here in the Bible to open the way for Paul, the same way John the Baptist opened the way for Jesus. It is simply a satanic imitation. And according to this same John, the Holy Spirit who was not yet in the world would have got Mary, the mother of Jesus pregnant.

See now what Paul, this spirit did in 1 Timothy 1, 20. 'Among these are Hymenaeus and Alexander, whom I have handed over to Satan to be taught not to blaspheme.'

See also 2 Timothy 2, 17 and 4, 14.

Here is another proof the Spirit of God was in the world long before this John of Paul and Paul. Read Genesis 6, 3. 'Then the Lord said, "My <u>Spirit</u> will not content with men forever, for he is mortal; his days will be a hundred and twenty years."'

So this is clearly contradicting what this John, this liar said in his gospel.

See again John 16, 13. 'But when he, the Spirit of truth, comes, he will guide you into all truth. He will not speak on his own; he will speak only what he hears, and he will tell you what is yet to come.'

I personally thing Jesus did just that. Now you know, now you're warned, so beware of what this Paul and the one who spoke for him said. For the ones who are not yet convinced about what I'm saying here about this John and the Jesus of this John, I will write especially for you.

See John 5, 31. 'If I (this John's Jesus) testify about myself, my <u>testimony is not valid</u>.'

See now this same Jesus in the same John's gospel. John 8, 14. 'Jesus answered, "Even if I testify on my own behalf, my <u>testimony is valid</u>, for I know where I came from and where I am going."'

Now you people, you must know that the Jesus who contradicted himself this way is not Jesus the true Prophet and the one who wrote this stories is not the John, the Jesus' apostle. They both are impostors in the Bible and this is the reason for me to write about these liars.

Paul calls names

See Acts 23, 2-3. 'The high priest Ananias commanded those standing beside him (Paul) to strike him on the mouth. Then Paul said to him, 'God is going to strike you <u>whitewashed wall</u>! Do you sit to try me according to the Law, and in violation of the Law order me to be struck?'

See now what the true Jesus said about this in Matthew 5, 22. 'But I say to you that anyone who is angry with his brother shall be guilty before the court; and who ever say to his brother, you good for nothing, should be guilty before the high court; and who ever says, you fool, shall be guilty enough to go into the fiery hell.'

I don't really know which one is worst; 'You fool' or; 'You whitewashed wall,' But I think neither should come out of the mouth of a Jesus' apostle toward his brother. So, according to Jesus, the true Prophet, Paul deserved to be judged before court, since he called them brothers also. Some people will tell me that Paul wasn't the judge's brother. Well, we'll see about that. Look in Acts 23, 1. 'Paul looked straight at the Sanhedrin and said: "My brothers, I have fulfilled my duty to God in all good conscience to this day."'

Paul called them, "Brothers just before he got mad and called the judge, "Whitewashed wall."

Paul had good conscience even after he mistreated Jesus' apostles and disciples and this long after his supposedly conversion to Jesus. You have to realize too that the ones who are my brothers are the ones who do the will of God. This is what Jesus said too. See Matthew 12, 50.

Paul called himself the father of many even though he didn't touch a woman.

See Philemon 1, 9-10. 'Yet I appeal to you on the basis of love. I then, as Paul—an old man and now also a prisoner of Christ Jesus—I appeal to you for my son Onesimus, who became my son while I was in chains.'

Jesus is fair, so, if you are prisoner, it means you're bad. Jesus did everything he did so we could be free, not prisoners. God is the Father of the living, but the devil who is a big imitator is also the father of many, but the father of lies, the father of the dead. See John 8, 44.

See Philemon 1, 12. 'Whom I have sent again: thou therefore receive him, that is, my own bowels.'

Bowels, these are intestines, aren't they? So, this is shit, isn't it?

See again Matthew 23, 8-10. 'But you are not to be called, 'Rabbi,' for you have only one Master and you are all brothers. And do not call anyone on earth 'father,' for you have one Father, and He is in heaven. (This is not Paul) Nor are you to be called 'teacher,' (deacon, priest, cardinal, bishop, pastor, pope) for you have one teacher, the Christ.'

This is not Paul either. But as I can tell, many have other than Jesus, the Christ as a teacher.

Each and everyone who disobey Jesus, the Christ's teaching, is antichrist. It is written in 1 John 2, 21. 'No lie comes from the truth.'

Do you really believe that a man coming from Jesus, the Christ, the true Prophet could have said and done so many things contrary to Jesus, the Saviour's teaching? I don't.

See 1 Corinthians 4, 14-17. Paul wrote: 'I am not writing this to shame you, but to warn you, as my dear children. Even though you have ten thousand guardians in Christ, you do not have many fathers, for in Christ Jesus (instead of Jesus Christ) I became your father (Jesus told his disciples they only have one Father and He is in heaven) through the gospel. Therefore I urge you to <u>imitate me</u>. (Jesus asked his disciples to be perfect like the heavenly Father is perfect) For this reason I am sending to you Timothy, <u>my son</u> whom I love, who is faithful in the Lord. He will remind you of <u>my way</u> of life in Christ Jesus, (not Jesus' way and not Jesus' teaching either) which agrees with what I teach everywhere in every church.'

And Jesus founded one and only one Church.

Paul is the father alright. He is the father of the demons out of hell to lie, to kill and to mislead people just like the devil did in the Garden of Eden.

This is enough to give me shivers in my back and make me sick to my stomach. We all know the devil is the one who like to imitate God the most and this only to mislead people. We also know he has begotten many children. God said about Jesus in Psalms 2, 7: 'I will proclaim the decree of the Lord: He said to me, "You are my Son; today I have become your Father."'

Now, this also means that Jesus became the Son of God the day God said he was and not before. That day God became Jesus' Father. This is the day Jesus left everything behind to do all and completely the will of God even if this meant to die because of it. This also meant Jesus loved God with his whole heart, his soul and with all of his thoughts.

It is true that the devil is a father and he has many children, in fact, he is the father of all who has sin just like Jesus said it. Jesus said that God is the Father of the living, meaning the Father of all without sin. John, Jesus' brother said basically the same thing. See 1 John 3, 3-10.

There are many false christs in this chapter. See 1, Corinthians 4, 16. 'Therefore I (Paul) urge you to imitate me.'

And unfortunately so many people did it.

See what Jesus, the true Prophet said in comparison in Matthew 5, 48. 'Therefore, be perfect as your heavenly Father is perfect.'

This means sinless.

See how the devil is described in 2 Thessalonians 2, 4. 'He will oppose and he will exalt himself over everything that is called God or is worshipped, so that he sets himself in God's temple, proclaiming himself to be God.'

This is what Paul did when he said, "Be my imitators."

See 1 Corinthians 4, 17. 'For this reason I (Paul) am sending you Timothy, my son whom I love, who is faithful in the Lord. He will remind you of <u>my way</u> of life in Christ Jesus, which agrees with what <u>I teach</u> everywhere in <u>every church</u>.'

See now what Jesus said in Matthew 16, 18. 'I will build my church (one church) and the gates of Hades will not overpower it.'

This is a great consolation to me. See that Jesus didn't say, 'Churches or every church.'

The only references I can find about every church or all the churches are in Paul's writing and his followers and no where else. You will find them from Acts 15, 41 to Revelation 22, 16. There is a good reason for someone to question.

Paul claimed to be a saint, he felt guilty of nothing that is bothering his conscience and who has begotten many. This is the exact description of Satan and his angels that were thrown out of heaven. It is not surprising that his successors are called; 'holy father' in Rome.

See again 1 Corinthians 4, 17. 'For this reason I (Paul) am sending you Timothy, my son whom I love, who is faithful in the Lord. He will remind you of my way of life in Christ Jesus, which agrees with what I teach everywhere in every church.'

There are two more things in this same verse that are not in accordance with the teaching of Jesus. Paul didn't ask his followers to remember the way of Jesus and neither the way of God, but the way of Paul. Paul had a very hard time to say, 'Our Lord Jesus Christ,' but he referred to Jesus as, 'Christ Jesus.' All the Jesus' apostles were more respectful of the name of their

Master and referred to him as, 'Our Lord Jesus Christ and not just, 'In Christ or for Christ or by Christ,' like Paul did. For your own reference, 'Christ Jesus and Jesus Christ are two different people.

This is quite a wish here from Paul in 1 Corinthians 7, 7. 'I wish that all men were as I am.'

Which means without women and without children, which would have meant the end of the world then if his wish came to reality, isn't it?

The king of false pride has spoken. This man was certainly not choking by humility.

Again Jesus' teaching is completely different. And he didn't say to be like him or to be his imitator, but to be perfect like his heavenly Father is. Paul seems to be the one Jesus talked about in John 5, 43. 'I have come in my Father's name and you do not accept me; but if someone else comes in his own name, you will accept him.'

We all know how much Paul is accepted, because who ever is responsible for it gave to Paul over ninety-five percent of the New Testament of the Bible. I personally think that the Paul's churches, the Christian Churches are largely responsible for this.

See Timothy 1, 18. 'Timothy, my son.' See also Galatians 4, 19. 'My dear children, for whom I am again in the pains of childbirth until Christ is formed in you.'

Wow! This must be very hard, very painful for a man to give birth to children. Maybe because Paul was best friend with Caesar, he might have got some caesareans.

Chapter 6

Paul fights against other disciples

We already saw how he fought against his brothers at his trial in Acts 23, 3.

His fight against Peter. I personally believe that what Jesus preached to us was dictated by God, the Father, the Almighty. So, Jesus is the one I have to listen to. In Matthew 18, 15 we can read: 'If your brother sins against you, go and show him his fault, just between the two of you.'

This story was to me the second clue that led me to find out who is the liar, the antichrist. My first clue was when I discovered that more than ninety-five per cent of the New Testament was written by someone else than Jesus' disciples and that it was written mainly by Paul and his followers.

Take a look if you want to in Galatians 2, 11-14. 'When Peter came to Antioch, I opposed him to his face, because he was clearly in the wrong. Before certain men came from James, (Jesus' brother) he used to eat with the Gentiles. But when they arrived, he began to draw back and separate himself from the Gentiles because he was afraid of those who belonged to the circumcision group. The other Jews joined him in his hypocrisy, so that by their hypocrisy even Barnabas was led astray.

When I saw that they were not acting in line with the truth of the (his) gospel, I said to Peter in front of them all, "You are a Jew, yet you live like a Gentile and not like a Jew. How is it, then, that you force Gentiles to follow Jewish customs?"'

The Jewish customs mentioned here are the Law of God, the commandments and the circumcision, an everlasting covenant between God and Abraham's descendants.

Paul said that Peter was in the wrong, but Paul did this mainly because Peter is the most considerate of all the apostles. Anyway, Paul's actions were not actions and neither words coming from a true Jesus' apostle or disciple. Paul said to Peter to his face and in front of everybody he was a hypocrite. Was the gospel written in those days anyway? I also doubt sincerely that Peter forced the Gentiles or anyone for this matter to be circumcised. He asked them maybe, but not forced them, but this story shows again how much Paul was against the circumcision, an everlasting covenant between God and his children. For sure the devil didn't want any of it.

See his fight also against Barnabas. Paul didn't digest and neither accepted that Barnabas joined Peter during this last fight.

Some of you would tell me that Paul was not Peter's brother. No, but it was Paul who pretended to be a Jesus apostle and Jesus said to his apostles they were all brothers. See again Matthew 23, 8.

By reading Paul's stories, we can see what kind of temper he had. We can certainly say he was not gentle and humble at heart.

See Acts 15, 39. 'They had such a sharp disagreement that they parted company. Barnabas took Mark and sailed for Cyprus.'

And we hardly heard about Barnabas after that. It was quite dangerous to contradict Paul and his army.

Here is what Jesus said to Peter in Matthew 19, 27-28. "Peter answered Jesus, "We have left everything to follow you! What then will there be for us?" Jesus said to them, "I tell you the truth, at the renewal of all things, when the Son of Man sits on his glorious throne, you who have followed me will also sit on twelve thrones, judging the twelve tribes of Israel."'

These words from Jesus to his apostles were good enough to make Paul jealous and Paul definitely couldn't wait for this day to judge others. Let me tell you that I too will be sitting with them, because I believe in Jesus and I follow his teaching, him who never quit saying we have to follow the Law of God, the commandments and to do the will of his Father who is in heaven. But then, this won't happen before the renewal of all things. Jesus also said that if we follow him we will never die. Don't be scandalized if I say, 'I follow Jesus of Nazareth; I follow the God of Israel.' When I say the same thing in French, people get scandalized; because I am and I follow translate the same way. You would be scandalized too if I say to you that I am Jesus of Nazareth or if I say that I am the God of Israel.

When Jesus said that we will never die if we follow him, he meant we will never commit a sin that causes us to die spiritually. These were not just words thrown in the air. At the exact moment your soul will leave your body, you will wake up, because it will be then no more time for you. Either it is six thousand years or an hour. Time exists only for those who are moving on this earth. The end of the world is nothing else than the separation of the evil ones from the righteous. The ones who commit evil won't be able to hurt the righteous anymore. This will mean paradise to the righteous and hell for the evil ones.

See Matthew 25, 31-33. 'When the Son of Man comes in his glory, and all the angels with him, he will sit on his throne in heavenly glory. All the nations will be gathered before him, and he will separate the people one from another as a shepherd separated the sheep from the goats. He will put the sheep on his right and the goats on his left.'

See Matthew 25, 41. 'Then he will say to those on his left, "Depart from me, you who are cursed, (all who have sins) into the eternal fire prepared for the devil and his angels."'

These are the ones who have sins and didn't want to repent. See also Matthew 7, 23. 'Then I will tell them plainly, "I never knew you. Away from me, you evildoers."'

Those my friends are those who say, "We all have sins and they are too proud to repent, which is the Jesus first recommendation. See Matthew 4, 17.

See also Jesus in Matthew 13, 41. 'The Son of Man (Jesus) will send out his angels, and they will weed out of his kingdom everything that causes sin and all who do evil.'

This means all who have sins. Jesus risked and gave his life to teach us these things, so do what God said about him in Matthew 17, 5. 'This is my Son, whom I love; with him I am well pleased. <u>Listen to him</u>!'

I believe my life will be in real danger the day other people will begin to believe what I say and begin following Jesus instead of Paul.

People who listen to Jesus do what Jesus said in Matthew 28, 19-20. 'Go therefore and make disciples of all nations, teaching them to observe all that I commanded you; and lo, I am with you always, even to the end of the age.'

This is exactly what I'm trying to do with my writing, my books and my songs.

You think just like I was thinking once that the Bible studies supplied by the churches are there to instruct you about the truth. Be careful, because when you'll know the truth, then you'll be ordered out the door. When this happens to you, then rejoice and be glad. The Bible studies of the Christian churches are in place to discover the ones who see the light, the ones who like me will be called disturbers in the assemblies. The ones who asked too many questions, especially the intelligent questions will be reprimanded and if they are persistent, then they'll show you the door. This will be a door closed in Paul's churches, but one door opened to the kingdom of heaven.

When you'll be talking about things that are not in line with the people who lead the Bible studies, you'll soon be the first to be shown the door. Just try and you'll see. When this happened to you, then be happy, because this will be to you a benediction, a great blessing.

I challenge anyone who goes to church to observe at any time the sermons you'll hear. You'll see they preach Paul at 99% and the rest, the one % about Jesus of Nazareth. This is just enough to make you believe they are preaching the right thing, the truth. Their god is not the God of Israel, but the god of Rome.

When they'll throw you out the door, don't cry, don't be sad, be happy, because you'll be closer to God than ever.

See Matthew 5, 11-12, 'Blessed are you when people insult you, persecute you and falsely say all kinds of evil because of me. (The word of God) Rejoice and be glad, because great is your reward in heaven, for in the same way they persecuted the prophets who were before you.'

The Jesus' messages are very nice, aren't they? Especially for the ones who listen to him, of course. You might think of joining another church, because it is so nice to hear the signing of those false hymns that sound so true, especially when we think they are made for the true God. Don't kid yourselves; the truth is not welcome in any of the Christian churches, because the truth will destroy them and they know it. This is very sad, but this is the way it is.

You go in different churches and ask them the same questions; you'll see how quick you'll be put in quarantine. Then, if you are persisting, they will tell all the other members of the congregation not to come near you and mainly not to talk to you. Do you see; the truth might be dangerous, contagious? It's not as bad as it was once. It was a time when people who speak like I do were burnt alive on a stake and accused of witchcraft. This is not this far behind either. Jesus also predicted this in his days. See Matthew 10, 17. 'Be on your guard against men; they will hand you ever to the local councils and flog you in their synagogues.' (In your churches)

It's bad enough, but not as bad as being handed over to Satan like Paul did.

Just a reminder here; don't forget these unspeakable actions were done mainly by Christians. Think of the crusades, the inquisitions and the wars against the Jews. Why those wars against the people of Israel, would you ask? The answers are very simple. One of the reasons is because Jesus would have said; see in John 4, 22. 'For salvation is from the Jews.'

I personally doubt the true Jesus said this. This in fact was a very strong provocation for jealousy to many people. The Jews' enemies are also God's enemies. Many wars are initiated by revenge.

There is a phrase, one of the biggest lie in the Bible spoken by Paul that Hitler used to incite his people to fight the people of Israel and you can read it in 1 Thessalonians 2, 14-15. 'You suffered from your own countrymen the same things those churches suffered from the Jews, who killed the Lord Jesus and the prophets and also drove us out. They displease God and are hostile to all men.'

On top of being one of the biggest lie it is a phrase that is one of the most anti-Semitic of the whole Bible and the world has to wake up.

Hitler, who is the most hated man, according to the Guinness World record book knew how to use this lie to convince his people that the Jews had to die and by the same token, he got the support of Rome in this war. Of course, both of them were following Paul, the devil. No one can honestly contest that Hitler was devilish. The result was that six million Jews died in the process.

Paul contradicts himself, contradicts Jesus and he contradicts God.

See the hypocrite in Romans 16, 1. 'I command to you our sister Phoebe, <u>a servant</u> of the church in Cenchrea.'

Well, my French Bible mentioned, 'A deacon,' instead of, 'A servant.'

Well, a deacon is a person who has the right to speak in the Christian churches. As far as I know, for what I learned from Paul's teaching, women have to keep their mouth shut in Paul's churches, don't they?

See 1 Corinthians 14, 34. 'Women should remain silent in the churches. They are not allowed to speak, but must be in submission, as the Law says.'

This phrase in itself must have kept thousands of women out of the churches or worst yet, away from the word of God. I think though the worse thing it did is giving men too much authority over women. For hundreds of years women were men's slaves and this was passed on from fathers to sons and this mainly because of Paul's teaching. One of the last men I argued against was telling me that Paul's teaching was good, is that right? How could we be this blind? He is crafty the enemy. Also, when this suits him well, then Paul and women are under the Law again. Believe me, they will be much better out of the Paul's churches the widows and all the women.

Here is what Jesus said about the Pharisees and the hypocrites like Paul and company. See Matthew 23, 14. 'Woe to you, scribes and Pharisees, hypocrites, because you devour widows' houses, and for a pretence you make long prayers; therefore you will receive greater condemnation.'

Did you see what it takes for a widow to be accepted as it in Paul's churches? See now what happens to the ones who are not sixty yet in 1 Timothy 5, 11-12. 'As for younger widows, do not put them on such list. (List of widows in need) For when their sensual desire (in need of a man) overcome their dedication to Christ, (Paul's churches) they want to marry. Thus they bring judgement on themselves, because they have broken their first pledge.'

In the mean time they can starve to death, according to Paul's teaching. I think the thorn in Paul's flesh was a bit of madness among other things. Here Paul said the widows bring judgement on themselves if they remarry, but see what he said in Romans 7, 2. 'By law a married woman is bound to her husband as long as he is alive, but if her husband dies, she is released from the law of marriage.'

See also 1 Corinthians 7, 39. 'A woman is bound to her husband as long as he lives. But if her husband dies, she is free to marry anyone she wishes, but he must belong to the Lord.'

I think what is following is the most defamation of the whole Holy Bible. This is a letter from Paul to his son

Timothy, him Paul, who said it's best to never touch a woman. See 1 Timothy 5, 9-10. 'No widow may be put on the list of widows unless she is over sixty, has been faithful to her husband, and is well known for her good deeds, (by the gossipers of the town) such as bringing up children, showing hospitality, <u>washing the feet of the saints</u>, helping those in trouble, and devoting herself to all kind of good deeds.'

If they don't fit in these categories, they can starve to death. In another word, if the widow didn't give a thousand times what she needs, she's not allowed to get help from Paul's churches. She has to be at least sixty. If she got married more than once, she is punished and banished. Woe to her if she didn't have the luck to bear children or if she is not recommended by the gossipers of the town. And even if she practiced hospitality, helped the ones in trouble and devoted herself to all kind of good deeds, if she didn't wash the feet of those saints, son of bitches, she is not allowed to receive help from the churches and this devil pretended to be a saint and millions others do too.

It is true that if a person believes in all this nonsense, those imbecilities, those lies and contradictions, it could very easily become crazy, as a priest once told my grand-father not to leave his children read the Bible. Take my word for it; the widows will be much better out of Paul's churches.

Paul couldn't foresee that we will have all this nonsense about him today; the abomination that causes desolation in the holy place, in the Holy Bible. We have to remember how Jesus described the devil in John 8, 44. 'A murderer, a liar and the father of lies.'

The leaders of Paul's churches do everything they can to hide the truth and they teach the lies and the contradictions, but their end will be the same than Paul's end. See Matthew 23, 33. 'You snakes! You brood of vipers! How will you escape being condemned to hell?

The Law that according to Paul was abolished and outdated is the Law that will judge him. See Ephesians 2, 15 and Romans 7, 6.

Paul Contradicts Himself and Jesus' Teaching

See 1 Thessalonians 5, 14. 'And we urge you brothers, warn those who are idle.'

See now 2 Thessalonians 3, 6. 'In the name of the Lord Jesus Christ, we command you, brothers, to keep away from every brother who walks disorderly and does not live according to the teaching you received from us.'

How nice this is? Paul commanded in the name of the Lord Jesus Christ to do the exact opposite of the Jesus' teaching. See Matthew 9, 12. 'On hearing this Jesus said, "It is not the healthy who needs a doctor, but the sick."'

The sick Jesus talked about here is the one who lives disorderly.

See also Matthew 18, 12. 'What do you think? If a man owns a hundred sheep, and one of them wanders away, will he not leave the ninety-nine on the hill and go look for the one that wandered off?'

So, as I can see, I have two different teachings in front of me here, I listen to Jesus, who are you listening to?

Now, I recommend you to follow Jesus' teaching here and to be very careful of what you're reading in 1 Thessalonians 4, 16-17. 'For the Lord himself will come down from heaven, with a loud command, with the voice of the archangel and with the trumpet call of God, and the dead in Christ will rise first. After that, we (Paul and his followers) who are still alive and are left will be caught up together with them (the dead in Christ) in the clouds to meet the Lord in the air. And so we will be with the Lord forever.'

Well. The Lord Jesus Christ said you will be thrown in the fiery furnace. You can listen and believe Paul if you want to, but I prefer and this by far listening and believing in Jesus Christ, the true Prophet, the one who tells the truth, so this way when the demons burn in hell, I'll be shining in the kingdom of my Father, just like Jesus said it.

See what I found while I was looking for the verses where the word Christ was taken according to me without respect, meaning; 'In Christ, by Christ, for Christ, etcetera.'

It is also proven the ones who are dead in Christ are lost, like the ones Paul said himself he will be with. See 1 Corinthians 15, 18. 'Then they also which are fallen asleep in Christ are perished.'

Lost, perished in the Bible really mean condemned to hell. Here we are; the letters to the Corinthians and the letters to the Thessalonians are from the same author, they are from Paul.

So Paul said it himself in his own letters that he is lost and he did everything he could to bring as many as possible down with him and seeing what happening around me with people who go to his churches, I got to say he succeeded on a big scale.

Did you notice that Paul said the dead in Christ will rise first. Well, I happen to know that my God is the God of the living, and Jesus told us so. I explained this mystery in another book called; Always and Forever.

We are not dead in Jesus Christ, we are alive. See Matthew 22, 31-32. 'But about the resurrection of the dead—have you not read what God said to you, 'I am the God of Abraham, the God of Isaac, and the God of Jacob'? He is not the God of the dead but of the living.'

The living is the one who lives his life without sin.

"Do you know what this means?" "It means God is the God of people like Abraham, Isaac and Jacob, the God of the righteous." "You're right, but it also means there is no resurrection for the dead, contrary to what Paul mentioned in 1 Thessalonians 4, 16-17. We are living in Jesus Christ, but they are dead with the false christ, the deceiver.

See what is written in John 11, 26. 'And whoever lives and believes in me (the word of God) will never die.'

See also John 6, 50. 'I am the living bread that came down from heaven, if anyone eats of this bread, he will live forever.'

Again, this bread is the word of God. See again Matthew 4, 4. 'Man does not live on bread alone, but on every word that comes out of the mouth of God.'

See also John 8, 51. 'I tell you the truth, if anyone keeps my word, he will never see death.'

This means my friends that if you keep the word of God and live by it; God will keep you away from the sin that causes death. Simple as that.

Jesus himself died on the cross, so this means he was speaking about the spiritual life. As I said it before, we are not dead in Jesus Christ, but we are alive. The dead are in the false christ and just like Jesus said it, he will send his angels to pull the weeds out and throw them in hell. In this case it is true Paul that you will be taken away.

Do you see that I'm not inventing anything, but I repeat the teaching of Jesus as he asked us to do? See again Matthew 28, 20.

See now Jesus in Matthew 13, 41-43. 'The Son of Man will send out his angels, and they will weed out of his kingdom everything that causes sin and all who do evil. They will throw them in the fiery furnace, where there will be weeping and gnashing of teeth. Then the righteous will shine like the sun in the kingdom of their Father.' This is the God of Israel, my Father.

This is very clear of what will happen to the one who keeps saying; 'We all have sins.'

Apparently the center of the earth is nothing but flames. Can you imagine living eternally in a volcano in eruption? See also what happened to the people who built a golden calf when Moses came down the Mount Sinai with the tables of the Law.

See also weeping and gnashing of teeth. There are no tears in the fire of two thousand degrees or more. So, this means hell will be pain well deserved but on earth. So wake up. God will gather all of his children, most likely the same way He did it when He commanded Moses to get his people out of Egypt. Please read Isaiah 35 for more info. When it comes to separate the truth from the lies, this day is here and this is something you can witness from your own eyes as I speak. Just remember also that God doesn't refuse anyone. It is the other way around. People are refusing to repent and to come to God.

Paul brags

This is false pride and vanity. Paul couldn't describe himself better than he did it in the following verse, and believe it, he knows it. See 2 Corinthians 11, 14-15. 'And no wonder, for Satan himself masquerades as an angel of light. It is not surprising then, if his servant masquerade as servants of righteousness. Their end will be what their actions deserve.'

Ho, because now for Paul deeds count. Let me show you again what Paul said about deeds. See Galatians 2, 16. 'Know that a man is not justified by observing the Law, but by faith in Jesus Christ. So we, too, have put our faith in Christ Jesus that we may be justified by faith in Christ and not by observing the law, because by observing the law no one will be justified.' (Or condemned)

See now what Jesus said about the deeds and, please correct me if I am mistaking by saying it is the total opposite. It is written in Matthew 16, 27. 'For the Son of Man is going to come in his Father's glory with his angels and then he will reward each person according to what he has done.'

Which really means his deeds, his actions, which is completely contrary to Paul's teaching, the liar.

If I was to write all the Paul's contradictions in the same book, this would be a book of at least one thousand pages and it would be illegal, because by men's laws, I'm only allowed to use one thousand verses from the Bible in one manuscript.

Also, if my book was of one thousand pages, you could very easily get tired of it and discouraged before you get to the end and by the same token, miss a lot of good messages. But don't go kill yourselves, because God is with you if you want Him and my writing is definitively an invitation to lead you towards Him. The vast majority of Jesus' messages, the Saviour asked us to turn to God and not to put our trust in mankind.

Please read with me 1 Corinthians 13, 4. 'Love is patient, love is kind, it does not envy, it does not boast, it is not proud. It is not rude, it is not self-seeking, it is not easily angered, it keeps no record of wrong. Love does not delight in evil but rejoices with the truth. It always protects, always trusts, always hope, always perseveres.'

It is hard to believe that 2 Corinthians 11, 16-30 was written by the same author.

I was not going to write 2 Corinthians completely, because I want to cut as short as possible, but it is too funny and I think you are ready for a good laugh. A Jesus' apostle is supposed to preach Jesus, what Jesus taught and what Jesus suffered to bring his teaching to us. Jesus also taught us to watch out for the false prophets that they are ferocious wolves. See Matthew 7, 15.

Here is what Paul was thinking of Jesus' apostles and his disciples in 2 Corinthians 11, 13. 'For such men are false apostles, deceitful workmen, masquerading as apostles of Christ.'

Here is Paul in 2 Corinthians 11, 16-30. 'I repeat, let no one take me for a fool. But if you do, then receive me just as you would a fool, so that I may do a little boasting. In this self-confident boasting I am not talking as the Lord would, but as a fool. (So, here Paul is saying he's talking as a fool.) Since many are boasting in a way the world does, I too will boast. You gladly put up with fools since you are so wise! In fact, you even put up with anyone who enslaves you (asks you to follow the Law of God) or exploits you or takes advantage of you or pushes himself forward or slaps you in the face. To my shame I admit that we were too weak for that! (See Acts 23, 2-3) What anyone else dares to boast about—I am speaking as a fool—(again) I (Paul) also dare to boast about. (Paul can't blame me for what I'm doing, because he said himself that he is a fool, that he speaks like a fool and that he is out of his mind.) Are they Hebrews? (Jesus' apostles) So am I. Are they Israelites? So am I. Are they Abraham's descendants? So am I. Are they servants of Christ? <u>I am out of my mind</u> to talk like this. (Again) I am more. I have worked much harder, been in prison more frequently, been flogged more severely, (Jesus told his apostles they will be. Paul should have stayed out of the synagogues and not talk to the Jews as he was not supposed to) and been exposed to death again and again. (Now, you have to understand here people that Paul is comparing himself to the Jesus' apostles. I was just wondering where and when he had the time to investigate what the Jesus true apostles were doing, and I continue with 2 Corinthians 11, 24.) Five times I received from the Jews the forty lashes minus one. Three times I was beaten with rods, once I was stoned, three times I was shipwrecked, I spent a night and a day in the open sea, I have been constantly on the move. I have been in danger from rivers, in danger from bandits, in danger from my own countrymen, in danger from Gentiles; in danger in the city, in danger in the country, in danger at sea; and in danger from false brothers. (Jesus' disciples. It's not all, but I could help it here and I have to bring in a commentary. It is hard or impossible to kill the devil) I have laboured and toiled and have often gone without sleep; I have known hunger and thirst and have often gone without food; I have been cold and naked. (I don't exactly know why, but I'm tempted to believe this last one.) Besides everything else, I face daily the pressure of my concern for all the churches. (Paul should have stayed with Jesus and take care of only one church) Who is weak and I do not feel weak? Who is led into sin and I do not inwardly burn? If I must boast, I will boast of the things that show my weakness.'

Paul said he suffered more than anyone and he accomplished more than anyone, that he worked harder than anyone and he would boast about his weakness???????

No matter what, it is not right to boast about oneself and Paul rather talked about himself and what he has done.

Paul couldn't really say he was a servant of Christ and he said he was out of his mind just to say he was more and he never talked about Jesus' suffering. Can you see that in Paul's writing you can hear a lot about Paul and not much about Jesus and Jesus' teaching? It is the same way in all the Christian churches, at least in the ones I have known.

Now you know why the Romans killed so many Jews from the years 67-73 and from 1939 to 1945 and many more that the information is not accessible to me.

Here in 2 Corinthians 11, 31, Paul is swearing again, which is taking God as a witness and to lie on top of all. It is actually a bad habit the liars use a lot. 2 Corinthians 11, 31. 'The God and Father of the Lord Jesus, who is to be praise forever, knows that am not lying.'

Now, if Paul was really from Jesus, he would have known what Jesus said and he would have listened to the Master. You can also see that the devil is not shy at all to use the name of God and the name of Jesus, God's servant to pass his messages; just the same way he did it in the Garden of Eden.

This is a very good one here in 2 Corinthians 12, 7. 'To keep me from becoming conceited because of these surpassingly great revelations, there was given me a thorn in my flesh, a messenger of Satan, to torment me.'

As if a messenger of Satan or Satan himself, who is the king of false pride would keep someone or anyone from becoming conceited. I think that the thorn in Paul's flesh was a bit of madness.

Here in 2 Corinthians we can see another clear imitation of Jesus by Paul. 'Three times I pleaded with the Lord to take it away from me.'

I'm asking you to reflect seriously on this one. Why would someone plead with the Lord, the true God to take away from him someone who wants to keep you from becoming conceited? Frankly, it's got to be someone devilish.

Remember Jesus' cup from Matthew 26, 39-44.

The more you will love God, the more He will be with you and the more He will be with you, the least the devil will have a hold on you, but the more he will try.

Read the story of Joseph and the story of Job. Oh, this doesn't mean that you won't suffer or never and that you won't have any affliction, because even Jesus wept over Jerusalem and even Jesus suffered from the evil men, but at the end you will be happy anyway.

See Matthew 5, 11-12. 'Blessed are you when people insult you, persecute you and falsely say all kinds of evil against you because of me. (The word of God) Rejoice and be glad, because great is your reward in heaven, for in the same way they persecuted the prophets who were before you.'

Believe Jesus, he knows it.

Paul Blasphemed

Paul Blasphemed before his so called conversion to Jesus, we know it, but I'll bring a reminder anyway. See 1 Timothy 1, 13. 'Even though I was once a blasphemer and a persecutor and a violent man, I was shown mercy because I acted in ignorance and unbelief.'

Him, Paul who studied with Gamaliel, the top, pleads ignorance. See Acts 22, 3-4. 'I am a Jew, born in Tarsus of Cecilia, but brought up in this city. (Jerusalem) Under Gamaliel I was thoroughly trained in the law of our fathers and I was just as zealous for God as any of you today. I persecuted the followers of this Way (Jesus' disciples) to their death.'

The law says; 'You shall not kill.' How could Paul pleaded ignorance, if not by lying and by hypocrisy?

See now what Paul did in Galatians 1, 8-9 and this was long after his supposedly conversion to Jesus. 'But even if we or an angel from heaven should preach a gospel other than the one we preached to you, let him be eternally condemned! As we have already said, so now I (Paul) say again, if anybody is preaching to you a gospel (full of lies and contradictions) other than what you accepted, let him be eternally condemned.'

Remember that Jesus came to teach, but not to judge and neither to condemn, but see, it is that Paul sat himself in God's temple, and for this reason he gave himself the right to judge, to condemn and to hand people over to Satan. See for yourselves 2 Thessalonians 2, 4.

Paul is ready to condemn an angel of heaven that would teach another gospel than his and we know now that his is full of lies and contradictions.

I think this is one of the worst blasphemies of the Bible. Only the devil or one of his hell angels is capable of such actions. Jesus asked us to forgive our enemies, not to condemn them. Maybe one day I'll have the time to count all the times in the Bible where Paul condemned and hand people over to Satan, which is the same thing. I only know this was a lot.

To realize that it is for the teaching of these lies and contradictions the Romans and all the responsible people have replaced the writing and messages of the true Jesus' apostles is troubling and disgusting. When Jesus was tempted by the devil in the desert, he told him to go away without condemning him. See Matthew 4, 1-11.

See also 2 Peter 2, 11. 'Yet even angels, although they are stronger and more powerful, do not bring slanderous accusations against such beings (demons) in the presence of the Lord.'

See also 2 Peter 2, 10. 'Bold and arrogant, these men are not afraid to slander celestial beings.' (God and his team.)

Paul makes people blind

I think this was Paul's first assignment, see Acts 13, 11. 'Now the hand of the Lord is against you. You are going to be blind, and for a time you will be unable to see the light of the sun. Immediately mist and darkness came over him, and he groped about, seeking someone to lead him by the hand.'

We know too now that Paul was also made blind, at least according to his own testimony, but can we believe what he said? See Acts 9, 8-9 and Acts 22, 11. Someone lied.

See what Jesus came to do on the earth in Matthew 11, 5. 'The blind receive sight, the lame walk, those who have leprosy are cured, the deaf hear, the dead are raised, and the good news preached to the poor.'

Just find me one message where Jesus punished someone. Yes, Jesus was opening the eyes of the blind and he is still doing this and he was condemning no one, because he came to save, not to condemn like Paul did it so many times. The ones who condemn and blind others are not sent by God or by Jesus, they are from the devil. Paul and his churches have shut down the eyes of people, not by hundreds, not by thousands, not by millions, but by billions and this still today. Neither God nor Jesus would have sent someone to blind someone, you can be sure of this.

Each time someone like me is trying to open people's eyes, there are thousands of others from churches, especially Christian who try to shut them up. They won't hesitate too, just like it happened in the pass to use men's laws to do it. The Jesus' disciples disturb the leaders of these churches, so they have to be eliminated. This is Paul's policy and also Jesus predicted this. See Jesus' message in Matthew 10, 18. 'On my account (on the account of the word of God) you will be brought before governors and kings as witnesses to them and to the Gentiles.'

Louis Riel was one of them, but this was fatal to him.

See also Titus 1, 10-11. 'For there are many rebellious people, mere talkers and deceivers, especially those of the circumcision group. (Who were working hand in hand with the Jesus' disciples.) They must be silenced.'

See revelation 11, 10. Two of God's prophets are tormenting the inhabitants of the earth. If the inhabitants of the earth are tormented, it's because when they hear the truth, they are confused, because all they knew were the lies they heard from their churches. I am pretty sure that people who will read my books will be tormented too and this is said without pretension, because I am only a Jesus' disciple. Also the ones who will accept the truth won't be tormented, but persecuted.

See Matthew 10, 27. 'What I tell you in the dark, speak in daylight; what is whispered in your ear, proclaim from the roof.'

Don't tell only your neighbours, but to all the nations. 'Many are invited, but few are chosen.'

Jesus needs me to tell all the nations and I need everyone who likes the truth to be known to help me with this challenge also. There are always people you can reach and I can't. God did a lot for you, but what have you done for Him?

Paul changes the Law

We already saw that Paul changed the Law about the last day of the week, the Sabbath in Acts 20, 7 and 1 Corinthians 16, 2.

We saw that for Paul to wait for the money was too much. He had to take the money and run. He had a very good racket, according to all the extravagant properties we can see in every town and village across the world, especially the st-Peter's Place in Rome. Don't worry though, all those properties will one day testify against all the crooks who took the money from the innocent people to build them.

My hope now is that a few of those who will read my books will love God with all their heart, soul and mind and their neighbour as themselves, enough to tell their neighbour the good news that the kingdom of heaven is very near. The kingdom of heaven is in the word of God. The kingdom is near and the judgement is near also, so make some Jesus' disciples and live forever an exciting eternal life. Why I published it? Because I love my neighbour as myself and I'm trying to do for you what Jesus did for me.

Let's hope you would like it and you will put the devil out of your life and by the same token, it opens for you the door of the kingdom of heaven. If someone can shut down the kingdom of heaven in people's face with their lies, this means someone else can open it for you with the truth.

Here is what Jesus said to the Pharisees like Paul and to all who are like him in Matthew 23, 33. 'You snakes! You brood of vipers! How will you escape being condemned to hell?'

See also Matthew 23, 13. 'But woe to you, scribes and Pharisees, hypocrites, (priests, bishops, archbishops, cardinals, popes and pastors and all of Paul's products) because you shut off the kingdom of heaven from people, for you don't enter it yourselves, nor do you allow those who are entering to go in.'

Very little has changed! One thing to notice too is that Jesus didn't condemn those snakes, bet he asked them how they could be saved. Jesus also said that the prostitutes and the tax collectors will enter the kingdom of heaven ahead of them. Let me tell you that the few prostitutes I talked to were drinking my teaching and that all of the church leaders rejected it.

I thank you very much for listening to me all of this time, because I know it is not easy to swallow so much in one time, but I also know that I'm running out of time to tell the entire world. You can always join me by Email at the following address; **Jamesprince@sasktel.net** if you have more questions for me.

Is there anyone among you who can tell me what he thinks of all this?" "Well, you're right; this is not easy at all to swallow."

"I should say that I am happy for discovering the truth and yet, I feel a very deep deception." "Are you disappointed for finding the truth or for have been lied to for all of those years?" "I'm not too sure. I feel like the sky suddenly fell on my head." "Well, if you got hit by heaven, you should recover very soon by accepting that heaven came to your rescue."

"Do you really think the day we serve God is important?" "What is important, according to my knowledge, is to obey God as our father Abraham did and so did Jesus, who told us that not the least stroke of a pan will disappear from the Law of God. See Matthew 5, 17-18. What would you say if I tell you that God doesn't listen to you on Sunday?" "I would say that we wasted a lot of time." "Who do you pray when you do?" "I pray Jesus who gave his life to save us." "Don't you think that if he gave his life to save us, we should at least listen to what he had to say? Please go read Matthew 6, 9." "'This, then, is how you should pray: "Our Father in heaven." '"

"If you pray anyone else than God, the Father, don't expect to be granted. Jesus also told us where to pray. Please read Matthew 6, 6." "'But when you pray, go into your room, close the door and pray to your Father who is unseen. Then your Father, who sees what is done in secret, will reward you.'"

"Jesus never said to pray him. Jesus always taught to pray the Father who is in heaven as he was doing himself and he always retrieved himself to do it, because it is one of the most private things to do. He had no room, no place to rest his head. As you can see now, all the answers are in Jesus' messages!" "But how come we don't seem to know these messages from Jesus?" "Maybe you should ask your Pastor for an answer."

"The truth is that I never really thought about it." "So Jesus was right as always when he said they were blind who lead the blind." "I must admit that there is a lot of the truth I didn't teach." "To teach the truth one must know the truth. But then, it is one thing not to teach the truth because we don't know it and another thing to hide it on purpose. Didn't you take a course before you started to teach?" "Yes, I spent four years in a Bible college." "Oh yes, there is the place where you learn not to talk about certain subjects that could maybe wake people up and make them enter the kingdom of heaven and because you need the whole congregation to make a living; you chose not to talk about them. It is hard to talk about things that could send people away from the church, isn't it? One has to love God and his word more than anything to teach the truth, otherwise we do what you do and teach the word of Paul, the lies, the word of the devil. You are also welcomed to contact me if you ever want to join Jesus' camp and learn to become a Jesus' disciple and in turn help others to become one too. The reward is worth a lot more than your salary. To tell you the truth, as always, I am very surprised that you had the patience to wait all of that time; which seems to me was a very long agony for you." "Well, I didn't really have the choice; I was more or less captive between a rock and a hard place." "It is not easy to argue against the word of God, that's for sure. We cannot forget either that we will be rewarded according to our actions or punished, contrary to what Paul said." "Where it is written again?" "This is written in Matthew 16, 27." "No one can say that you don't know the word of God, that's for sure." "I know it and I eat it, just like Jesus suggested it in Matthew 4, 4 and I am happy I could make you eat a bit of it today too. Although, it is more than time I leave you now and I repeat it, this was a real pleasure for me to help you open a new chapter in your life."

"Thank you very much sir for coming here to give us the word of God today." "Thank God instead that allowed such a blessing to you. As for me, you are very welcomed.

Everything is recorded and I give you the permission to make as many copies as you wish. Have a good day now. I should go see my mother now before she starts worrying too much. A mother is always a mother; as you know and we all have to honour her, no matter our age.

CHAPTER 7

Of course my mother had a lot of questions for me on my return. She would have liked to come to the assembly too, but poor her, she can hardly hear anything anymore and this is harder on her than her missing leg. Her leg doesn't make her suffer anymore, but not being able to hear makes her suffer every day. One thing though that has never left her is curiosity.

"How did they react? Have you been booed? I am sure the pastor didn't like your intrusion. Did they let you speak at least?" "Would you leave me a chance to answer one of your questions at least?" "Excuse me, but I am very anxious to know how this turned out." "Yes I spoke and I did it for a long time, maybe too long. As you already know, there is a lot to say, a lot more than it can be done in a few hours. Although I think I might have touch a few of them. I'm sure you will hear about it very soon. I think some are for it, some are against it and others are not too sure. If I rely on what Jesus said, one out of two received the truth with joy and the other half will reject it. It is written in Matthew 14, 40. 'Two men will be in the field; one will be taken and the other left. Two women will be grinding with a hand mill; one will be taken and the other left.'

Jesus who knew what he was saying kept the same talk all along his ministry. Remember what he said about the father will be against his son, the mother against her daughter and so on. This too is written in Matthew. I think it is in Matthew 10, 35.

One thing is sure and this is if Jesus said it we can and we must believe it." "You seem to have a lot or a blind trust in Matthew?" "If it wasn't for Matthew, we would have very little or next to nothing of the truth, but my trust in Matthew is not blind at all. There are things in Matthew too that are not in accordance with the word of God and as you yourself often said; we have to have good judgement and discernment." "I thought from hearing you that Matthew was completely reliable, very solid." "Mom, you know that the weeds Jesus talked about in Matthew 13 are true for all that is written and this is why Jesus told us to be careful when we read." "Can you give me a few examples of what you mean?" "Of course I can do it. To start with, we have to look in Matthew 12, 31. 'And so I tell you, every sin and blasphemy will be forgiven men, but the blasphemy against the Spirit will not be forgiven.'

Do you see mom? God is Spirit and the two are One and the same and every sin and every blasphemy are against God and against his Spirit. Jesus, the true Prophet didn't come to judge or to condemn, but to save. But in this message, this Jesus is condemning just about everybody, just like Paul did it, which is completely ridicules, completely non sense; which means completely impossible too. Jesus who would leave the ninety-nine sheep on the hill to go save the one that is lost has never said such abomination. This verse is either from Paul or from one of his disciples, maybe John's Paul who talked about the Counselor to come. See John 16, 13." "You said there are other examples?" "Another one that comes to my mind at this minute is the one where Jesus basically denies being the son, the descendent of David, which is also impossible, because this would make Jesus a liar. Go read Matthew 22, 45." " 'If then David calls him 'Lord,' how can he be his son?'"

"If Jesus is not the son of David like these lines seem to say; which means a direct descendant of David, he simply can't be the Messiah, the king of the Jews like the true Jesus said he is when he was questioned before Pilate and also according to all the prophets who were there before Jesus. Again, the Jesus who is in Matthew 22, 45 is not the true Jesus; he is an impostor, a fake. I'm sure of it. We cannot forget either that Jesus, the true Prophet has been called Son of David hundreds of times before without him denying it even once." "I am tempted to believe you on this one. Do you think there is more?" "There are a few more things that are bothering me, yes." "What are they?" "Before I go any farther I would like to come back talking about the sin against the Spirit and remind you that God who is also Spirit asked us to forgive to others all their sins if they repented. Now, to answer your question, I would simply tell you that I doubt very much that Jesus told who the trader was among his apostles at the last supper, where they were all together and if Jesus did it, there would have been there at least a huge discussion about it and Matthew would have talked about it too. We cannot forget either what Jesus said about having a problem between two of them in Matthew 18, 15. 'If your brother sins against you, go and show him his fault, just between the two of you.'

I just know that the true Jesus wouldn't have acted contrary to his own teaching and Judas showed to all of them he was the trader when he kissed Jesus accompanied with the soldiers to arrest Jesus." "You're right about this one too. Jesus wouldn't have acted contrary to his own teaching. I'm sure of it too. So there are weeds, some lies and contradictions in the gospel of Matthew too." "Yes, but Matthew has nothing to do with it. He is crafty the enemy and he did everything possible to deceive and I can also said too now that he succeeded just as well as he did in the Garden of Eden with Adam and Eve and this despite all of Jesus and God's warnings. I don't exactly know why, but it seems to me that the world has the tendency to listen to the devil instead of listening to God. It is true that the devil is a seducer and I would call him also a faller. Many get caught in his trap, the body is weak." "I hope this is all the weeds there are in the gospel of Matthew." "There is more mom and the worse is coming." "This is incredible, but how could you find all this?" "I have only one explanation and this is that God has opened my eyes, but what ever happens mom, don't you ever let someone say that I'm a saint, because Jesus said it himself that, 'Only One is good.' And he was not talking about himself, but about the Father who is in heaven. Read if you don't mind what is in Matthew 19, 16-17." "'Now a man came up to Jesus and asked, 'Teacher, what good thing I must do to get eternal life?' 'Why do you ask me about what is good?' Jesus replied. 'There is only One who is good. If you want to enter life, obey the commandments.' 'The Law.

This is a very convincing message from Jesus and it is contradicted by Paul in many places in the Bible, especially in the New Testament.

There is another abomination in the Bible that I think could also be one of the worse and this is the way the conception of Jesus, supposedly by the Holy Spirit was presented to the world. See mom, God was so upset with people of the earth at the time of Noah that He almost destroyed it all with the flood. Do you know mom the main reason for God to be this mad with his creation?" "I think it was because of the out of hand corruption."

"Let me read to you the main reason for God to send the flood and this is in Genesis 6, 2-7. 'When men began to increase in number on the earth, and daughters were born to them, <u>the sons of God</u> saw that the daughters of men were beautiful, and they married any of them they chose. Then the Lord said: "My Spirit will not contend with man forever, for he is mortal; his days will be a hundred and twenty years." The Nephilim were on the earth in those days—and also afterward—when the sons of God went to the daughters of men and had <u>children with them</u>. They were the heroes of old, men of renown. The Lord saw how great man's wickedness on the earth had become, and that every inclination of the thoughts of his heart was only evil all the time. The Lord was grieved that He had made man on the earth and his heart was filled with pain. So the Lord said: "I well wipe mankind, whom I have created, from the face of the earth—men and animals, and creatures that move along the ground, and birds of the air—for I am grieved I have made them."'

I'm telling you mom, it is because of a righteous man, because of Noah that we are very lucky to be here today.

Anyway, God was so mad against his sons, his angels because they went with the daughters of men and had children with them that He thought of destroying everything on the face of the earth and this includes mankind and He would have done the same thing with Mary, Jesus' mother????? I don't think so.

If I understand right here; we are talking about angels, spirits that had sexual desire. It is possible to talk about those things today because the knowledge of the most has increased. See Daniel 12, 4.

We don't need to be genius of the science or a university student to know today that we are witnesses of this phenomenal. And even the scientists don't speak about all these things I'm talking about in this book. It is most likely because they don't know about it and if they know and don't talk about it, I would call this cowardice.

You can find this abomination in Matthew 1, 18. 'This is how the birth of Jesus Christ came about: His mother Mary was pledged to be married to Joseph, but before they came together, she was found to be with child through the Holy Spirit.'

This is the Spirit that according to the John of the gospel of John was not in the world yet. See John 14, 26, 'But the Counselor, the Holy Spirit, whom the Father will send in my name, will teach you all things and will remind you of everything I have said to you.'

See also John 7, 39. 'By this he meant the Spirit, whom those who believed in him were later to receive. Up to that time the Spirit had not been given, since Jesus had not yet been glorified.'

What a crap, what a lie! Jesus was baptizing everybody he met with the Holy Spirit. See Matthew 3, 11. 'As for me, (John the Baptist) I baptize you with water for repentance, but he who is coming after me (Jesus) is mightier than I, and I am not fit to remove his sandals, he will baptize you with the Holy Spirit and fire.'

See Exodus 31, 3. 'I (God) have filled him (Isaac) with the Spirit of God, in wisdom.'

See Luke 2, 25. 'Now there was a man in Jerusalem called Simeon, who was righteous and devout. He was waiting for the consolation of Israel, and the Holy Spirit was upon him.'

There are many more proofs the Holy Spirit was in the world and with some people and when this liar says He is not yet given, well, I'm insulted. That the Holy Spirit wasn't with this liar, this John, I can see and understand that. Understand that we are not talking about the true John of the true Jesus here.

It was shortly after this that Paul came into the picture. He is crafty the enemy.

It is a sure thing that God, the Father wanted that a son is born to Mary and that he becomes the Messiah, which means the one who will announce to all the nations of the earth the word of God, the will of God, because He said He will raise a Prophet from the brothers of Israel and He did it. See Deuteronomy 18, 18.

It is a sure thing also that God allowed that Jesus was born, but from allowing Jesus to be born and fertilizing his mother, there is a world or two. This Prophet is Jesus. He did his job and did it well and Paul, the devil did everything in his power to destroy God's plan, which means Jesus' work. Should we expect anything else from the devil after knowing all of Jesus' warnings?

At the beginning of the gospel of Matthew we can read: 'The genealogy of Jesus. A record of the genealogy of Jesus Christ, <u>the son of David</u>, the son of Abraham.'

I am sorry if I repeat it again, but for Jesus to be the true prophet, the true Messiah who was announced by other prophets long before his birth; he has to be a direct descendant of David, just like his genealogy said he is in Matthew. Read carefully Matthew 1, 16. 'And Jacob the father of Joseph, the husband of Mary, of whom was born Jesus, who is called Christ.'

As you can notice yourselves; neither God or the Holy Spirit is mentioned in the genealogy of Jesus in Matthew or in Luke.

God is mentioned as the Father of Adam in the Jesus' genealogy of Jesus in Luke 3, 37.

God didn't need a woman to make Adam and neither a woman to raise a prophet in Israel. We all know how Adam was created.

To be the king of the Jews like Jesus confirmed himself he is, he has to be a direct descendant of King David. See Matthew 27, 11. 'Meanwhile Jesus stood before the governor, and the governor asked him, "Are you the king of the Jews?" "Yes, it is as you say," Jesus replied.'

Jesus is really the king of the Jews as a man. There are two things that are essential to become a king of Israel as much as King David and King Solomon were. A man had to be a direct descendant of King David and he has to be anointed by God." "All this is not easy to understand at all." "On the contrary mom, all you have to do is believing in Jesus who said the truth and the lies will be together until the end of the ages. It is written in Matthew 13, 30. 'Let both grow together until the harvest.'

The righteous and the evil ones will be together until the end, until the judgement. Jesus said the harvest is the end of the ages and this is why I know we are at the door, because the truth is getting separated from the lies." "But I thought it is the angels that Jesus will send who are supposed to pull out the weeds, the lies." "If you are careful when you read mom; as Jesus asked us to do in Matthew 24, 15, you will see that the angels will weed out everything that causes sin and all who do evil. I don't do the same thing; I am gardening by separating the weeds from the wheat, the lies from the truth. This is not quite the same thing." "You are right then; we have to be careful when we read." "It is good to listen to Jesus in everything, especially what he said in Matthew 24, 15, because when we know the truth we can reject the lie if we love God.

Let me know the commentaries your friends will have about all this, would you? I am very curious about it. You know, this was kind of my first time in one of these churches for teaching. I'm glad I could get out of there without being too bashed out. I think though that some of them will be disturbed, at least for a while. This is what happens when we refuse to believe the Bible is made out of both, weeds and wheat, the truth and lies.

It is kind of strange though, because it's Jesus, the true Prophet, the Son of God who said it and very few people believe me when I mention it. They tell me the Bible is holy and it contends nothing else than the truth, the word of God. As if it could be God who blasphemes against an angel of heaven for teaching a different gospel full of lies and contradictions like Paul's gospel. See Galatians 1, 8-9.

In any cases mom, I think I gave my audience and my readers something to reflect about many points of the Bible." "I am very concern about what your enemies could do to you; knowing what happened to Jesus." "There is nothing I could do about this, but don't you worry; I put my destiny in the hands of God and He is the Master of my future."

My mom and I had a hard time finishing our meal, because phone calls kept coming in. Some of them to say that I had a good teaching even if this was a shock for most of them. Others called to say that I was no one other than the antichrist and wanted to make sure my mom doesn't talk to them anymore. When I saw mom coming back to the table with tears in her eyes, I got up and I went to disconnect the phone line to have peace at least for the time of the meal. After lunch I reconnected the phone, but I sat close to it with the intention to answer it myself. Of course this was very disturbing for her, but I was certainly not going to leave those wolves devour her alive as they wished they could do without me doing anything.

"Hi, can I speak to Mr. James Prince please?" "You are talking to him. What can I do for you?" "Do you really believe it is God who speaks to you when you are dividing people the way you do?" "Me, dividing people? It's the other way around; I do all my best to reunite people around the word of God, just like Jesus did it. Do you have access to a Bible?" "Of course I have a Bible, I spend most of my days reading in this book that I adore." "Do you mind please open it and read what is written in Matthew 10, 35." "'For I have come to turn a man against his father, a daughter against her mother, a daughter-in-law against her mother-in-law—a man's enemies will be the members of his own household.'

But it is written basically the opposite in Matthew 5, 9. 'Let me read it to you if you allow me." "Of course, go ahead." "'Blessed are the peacekeepers, for they will be called sons of God.'"

"This is exactly what Jesus did with his ministry. Nobody can be more in peace with himself and with God that I am. This is said without any pretension, because this is not because of my deeds, but because of my love for the truth. Can you see that Jesus knew that within a family some members will believe the truth and others will not; which brings undeniably some divisions? This is what happens in my own family too. Very few believe the truth and many believe in Paul's lies, in their religions and its slavery. They will be blind for as long as they don't receive love for the truth. 'Seek and you will find.' Jesus said it and when you'll get it; you too will have peace in your heart and in your mind and you will quit wondering for yourself and like me you will try to make the truth known to others and you too will meet resistance the same way I do." "So then, I have to keep looking?" "I gave you a lot of clues this morning that will help you finding the truth and it is up to you from now on to keep looking and I'm sure you will find. Always keep in mind though that everything and anything that contradicts the teaching of Jesus and contradicts God is antichrist and only the truth, the word of God will show you this. When Jesus, the word of God will become your Master, see Matthew 23, 8-10, you wouldn't call anyone, 'father or pastor' anymore,' because only one then will be your Master, the Christ, the word of God and only one will be your Father and this will be the one who is in heaven."

"Who was this?" "This was someone who was at the assembly this morning and she seems to be confused and looking for the truth. The only fact she's looking means she will find." "I will never see the end of this" "If you too mom want to be worthy of the word of God; you too have to carry your own cross. Jesus said it and you can read it in Matthew 10, 38. 'And anyone who does not take his or her cross and follow me is not worthy of me.'

This is why I often say that I follow Jesus of Nazareth; I follow the God of Israel; which brings me to a song I composed called;

I follow Jesus, I follow God

This title is confusing a lot for French people, because I follow and I am translates the same way. What would you say if you hear me say: I am Jesus of Nazareth; I am the God of Israel? The song is not made in English, but I would like to translate it for you.

I follow Jesus of Nazareth, the one they crucified
I follow the true Prophet, he who tells us the truth
I follow the God of Israel, He who created everything
I am his faithful child, I follow his given Law
I have to be careful; they will put me in jail
For telling this truth, I'll be persecuted
This is what Jesus predicted to who follows him
We are like sheep among ferocious wolves

We'll have to flee this kind or they will flog me
And to go up to the end, I'll have to love with no end
Not to fear for my body I will not see death
Because the One who has my soul saved it from hell
Be careful when you read all the written words
They can be misleading, the Lord said it
Listen to Him and be ready, his coming is near
We don't know the day or the hour said the Lord
I follow Jesus of Nazareth, the one they crucified
I follow the true Prophet, he who tells us the truth
I follow the God of Israel, He who created everything
I am his faithful child, I follow his given Law
I follow Jesus of Nazareth.

"This can be very confusing my son," "Will be confused only who ever is refusing to accept the truth. The one who accepts the truth will be happy to say and to sing along with me that there is no better joy than to see and to live in the kingdom of heaven and to follow and Jesus and God." "Don't you think that we have to die to enter the kingdom of heaven?" "Mom, you are mistaking the kingdom of heaven with the kingdom of God." "Do you mean this is not the same thing?" "Not at all and Jesus made a lot of efforts to show us the difference. They are two different kingdoms and in two different times. The kingdom of heaven is like a fish cleaned out of its guts, just like a person is cleaned out of his sins. This can only happens with the repentance and is what Jesus preached right from the beginning of his ministry. Look for yourself in Matthew 4, 17." "'From this time on Jesus began to preach, "Repent for the kingdom of heaven is near." '"

"Of course the kingdom of heaven was near and is still near, it is in the word of God. When Jesus said the scribes and the Pharisees, the priests and all the leaders are shutting down the kingdom of heaven in people's face, that they don't let enter who wants to enter and they don't enter themselves, it is because they hide the truth to people, to the world. When Jesus gave to Peter the keys of the kingdom of heaven, it was because Peter knew the truth, the word of God and live by it. The word of God, the truth opens the doors of the kingdom of heaven. If you listen to me you will know the truth and you will see the kingdom of heaven as well. I don't tell things that are from me, but some messages that are from Jesus, meaning from God. Think about it for a minute mom; do you really think someone can stop anyone from entering the kingdom of God? Although, if it's the truth that allows us to enter the kingdom of heaven and that someone hides the truth, then yes, this someone can shut down the kingdom of heaven in people's face, just like Jesus said it. It is written in Matthew 23, 13. 'Woe to you teachers of the law and Pharisees, you hypocrites! You shut the kingdom of heaven in people's faces. You yourselves do not enter, nor will you let those enter who are trying to.'

This is what the leaders of those religions do by hiding the truth to people; they're forbidding their people from seeing the kingdom of heaven. This a formal proof they are following Paul, the liar instead of following Jesus who did everything possible to open the kingdom of heaven to people with the truth that comes from God. Again, no leader will be able the shut the kingdom of God to people either they lie or not.

When people like Jesus and Louis Riel do everything they can to make the truth known, well, you already know what happened to them. It is no doubt what I can expect too. I made a song about the kingdom of heaven too, but it is in French only for now. If you want to, I will translate it for you." "You know that I like your songs." "In the matter of fact, it's called;

The Kingdom of Heaven?
Have you seen the kingdom of heaven?
It's in the teaching of Jesus.
It's nice, it's great and it's marvellous
If you believe, how come you didn't see it?
You have to be born again
To see it and to see how nice it is
The kingdom is the nicest pearl
It's for me my ticket for heaven
God took away evil from my life
And allowed me to live very happily
What I have, Jesus promised it,
To whoever leaves everything to be with God
Jesus is the one with the truth
And his word won't cheat you
Go see what he says in Matthew
He alone spoke about this kingdom
I found this precious pearl
It is one of the greatest values
There is no truth better than the truth
This is why Jesus called the sinners
Because of sins they are prisoners
Repentance is the only way out
Jesus told us the truth
Listen to him as God told us to do
Have you seen the kingdom of heaven?
It's in the teaching of Jesus.
It's nice, it's great and it's marvellous
If you believe, how come you didn't see it?
You have to be born again
To see it and to see how nice it is
To my God I gave everything
To have it for the eternity."

"You're right by saying the kingdom is great and your song is great too" "The whole truth from God is great mom and I don't understand why so many members of our family don't want to accept it. I thought for a long time they all love God and the truth as much as I do. No one can say loving God and reject the truth from God at the same time. This would be hypocrisy and we all know what Jesus said about it." "We have to give them time; it is not given to everyone to understand and to believe the right thing." "Oh, I don't thing they're not believing, I just thing they believe in the lies as I did too for too many years. I though quitted believing the lies when I discovered the truth. It is one thing not knowing the truth, but it is a different thing to reject it, to refuse to look for it and not loving it. God's children only live by it." "Are we not all God' children?" "Jesus told us God is the God of the living, which means the God of people who lives with no sin." "But I thought we all have sins" "This is what Paul and company made people believe and because the body is weak, well, we believed that.

Although, when we have sincerely repented of all our sins; then sin is no longer with us and we are washed out; just like a fish ready to be eaten. This is what the kingdom of heaven is like, just like Jesus described it. It's good to feel clean." "Where did you see that we are no longer the children of God when we have sins?" "Just like the sin of Adam and Eve caused their spiritual death and they were separated from God for a time; it is the same for everyone who sins. God told them that if they disobey, they will certainly die. Now, if you read 1, John 3, 9-10, you will see that there are two families. 'No one who is born of God will continue to sin, because God's seed remains in him; he cannot go on sinning, because he has been born of God. This is how we know who the children of God are and who the children of the devil are:

Anyone who does not do what is right is not a child of God; nor is anyone who does not love his brother.'

As you can see mom; there are really two families and God is the Father of the ones who live without sin and the devil is the father of the sinners. Jesus told us that we cannot serve two different masters, so either we serve God or we serve the devil, simple as that. If you sin you are pleasing the devil and if you don't then you are with your God, your Father. There is nothing complicated in this statement. When we love God with all of our heart, with all of our soul and with all of our thoughts, we hate sins, which ever it is. To do so we have to love God more than ourselves and this is what makes us worthy of his word. This is actually the recipe Jesus gave us to obtain eternal life. In Matthew 22, 37-38, Jesus told us this is the first and the greatest commandment. In another occasion Jesus told us that observing the commandments is the way to obtain eternal life. It is in Matthew 19, 17. 'If you want to enter life, obey the commandments.'

Of course the devil told us the exact opposite, because his goal is always to deceive, to mislead. It's him who said that we are not under the law anymore; that we are under the grace. I guess this seems true enough the make billions of people swallow the pill. The sinners are saying they are under the grace and they say they all have sins. What kind of grace is this, really?"

Then the phone rang again, interrupting our conversation, but this time it was one of my sisters who was calling to say she and another sister visiting her will be at mom soon. They weren't very long, because within fifteen minutes they were both of them in a big discussion with me. While Diane was busy contradicting me on everything I was saying; Carolle started to read one part of this manuscript left on the table near her.

I was just telling Diane the huge surprise she will get when she'll wake up one day and of course she argued that on the contrary it will be me who will get the shock. Although I just know that if I preach Jesus and Jesus' teaching, I just can't be mistaking, I can't be wrong while she believes strongly in Paul.

There is when Carolle got up suddenly with a fit that I have never seen in her before and I think this is when she read: 'Je suis Jésus de Nazareth, je suis le Dieu d'Israël.' Which means; 'I follow Jesus of Nazareth, I follow the God of Israel. But this also means; 'I am Jesus of Nazareth, I am the God of Israel.

I follow Jesus and the Bible proves it. It is a sure thing though that the truth can be shocking.

Carolle still in her fit headed out the door calling Diane to come out too if she didn't want to walk and that the walk was quite long. Jesus said a prophet is not welcome in his own family and I can say with proofs that a Jesus' disciple is not welcome either.

I have some ideas of what he had to go through himself. Jesus never talked much about his parents and brothers. He said his brothers, sisters and mothers were the one who do the will of his Father in heaven. See Matthew 12, 50. 'For whoever does the will of my Father in heaven is my brother and sister and mother.' This is what I say too.

This is what Jesus said when he was told his mother and brothers were waiting to talk to him.

Some members of my own family are just one step away to make another one of Jesus' prophesy come through and it's written in Matthew 10, 21. 'Brother will betray brother to death and a father his child; children will rebel against their parents and have them put to death.'

My son rebelled against me and he didn't talk to me for more than six years now.

See Matthew 10, 17. 'Be on your guard against men; they will hand you over to the local councils and flog you in their churches.'

My own brother who is not my brother in Jesus suggested calling the police after receiving a slap he deserved at least a hundred times and ten times weaker than it should has been. I think he never learned respecting my birthright after all and Jesus told us to look for justice. See Matthew 5, 6. 'Blessed are those who hunger for righteousness, (justice) for they will be filled.'

My brother told me in a very arrogant way and this at six inches from my nose that I have never studied the Bible in my entire life. The temptation was just a bit too great and I couldn't resist. He got up then and he tried to put me down, but I asked him to stop, because I didn't want to distress our ninety years old mom any longer, but he didn't want to. He just wanted to put me down and he continued wrestling, but of course, I too learned how to dance the tango. I offered him to come outside if he wanted to continue, but he wouldn't come anywhere where mom couldn't protect him anymore. It is then he has suggested calling the police. I told him he was coward enough to do this. Mom agreed with him, but it was mainly to protect her baby son who is over two hundred pounds big boy she was afraid he gets hurt. It is very sad for her, but neither God, nor Jesus like the hypocrisy and to be convinced of it, one only have to read Matthew 23.

Jesus said we will be filled and I am. I only have one little regret about this story and this is I wished I had given it to him just the way he deserved it, but God also said: See Deuteronomy 32, 35. "It is mine to avenge."

Jesus asked us to chase demons, but as far as I know, he didn't tell us which weapon to use to do it. I can think of prayers. I just hope I chased a few of those demons out of my brother's head, out of his heart. A slap is a lot less than if I used a twenty-two rifle.

Then I told this brother of mine that according to this Paul; he and so many Christians want to defend and protect, he is condemned, because Paul condemned everybody, even Jesus' disciples and even Jesus and even an angel of heaven. You can read it in many places in the Bible, but particularly in 1 Corinthians 6, 9-10. 'Do you not know that the wicked will not inherit the kingdom of God? Do not be deceived: Neither the sexually immoral nor idolaters nor adulterers nor male prostitutes nor homosexual offenders nor thieves nor the greedy nor drunkards nor slanderers nor swindlers will inherit the kingdom of God.'

It is a matter of fact the devil wants them all. Paul didn't mention the murderers and the liars or blasphemers, what he is and also, if he was preaching Jesus' gospel, he too would have talked about the kingdom of heaven instead of the kingdom of God.

My brother and all the others can contradict me all the want, but Paul here is condemning all these people to hell, which is for all who don't enter the kingdom of God. But I say the same thing Jesus said; that there is only one way to be saved and this is by repentance and if there is another one, it would be to turn away from sin. 'Go and live your life off sin.' Jesus said.

Trying to save people from hell is a bit like trying to save someone from drowning. He lost his mind and he won't hesitate to put you down under the water in the hope of saving himself; not realizing that by killing his rescuer, he condemns himself to death.

When he heard this story one man I know asked me if my brother turned out the other cheek. Of course I had to tell him the truth that was the other way around. My brother didn't and neither did Paul. See Acts 23, 3.

On the contrary, my brother jumped me and tried to put me down, contrary to Jesus' teaching that you can read in Matthew 5, 39. 'If someone strikes you on the right cheek, turn to him the other also.'

I know too that with my temper I would most likely have done the same thing. I never let anyone step on my big toe or let anyone hit me without defending myself when I was attacked, but I rarely look for trouble and I never ran away from a fight.

We have to understand here that a slap in a man's face in those days was an invitation to a dual to death, which of course Jesus was against. But I am certain that not too many men would turn his cheek a second time if he is slapped by a man like Mike Tyson.

I don't know if it matters or not, but Jesus mentioned the right cheek and I slapped my brother on the left one. It is true that he was mean by talking to me like he did, but I should have listened to Jesus and not resisted him. I should have listened to Jesus and shook the dust off my feet and get out of this house, because they don't want to listen to my words, but this is not an easy thing to do in your mother's home. She is grieved enough as it is with what happened. To tell you the truth, I must say that the slap went as fast as the insult came; it was not a premeditated action at all.

It is true that from many people point of view, trying to save someone who doesn't want to be, despite his will is a bit of foolishness, but Jesus did it and I follow him and I'm trying to do the same.

Although the whole situation kind of put a tragic and brutal end to a trip that has started fairly well.

I took a bus from the Montreal Airport to Victoriaville on which I slept for most of the ride, but from Drummondville on I was completely woken. It is then I started a conversation with the driver. I was sitting on the front seat and I said: 'There must have been a lot of good people in Quebec with all these names of saints along the road, isn't it?' The driver answered: "Yes, and some of them are very rare and damned hard to pronounce." "The only fact they had to carry a name like this all their life was enough to be called; 'Saint.'"

Then the woman sitting on the front seat, just behind the driver joined the conversation too. We had this in common, we both had a front seat. I could tell she was thirsty for the truth, which is quite rare in the Christian churches nowadays and I think this is the main reason why they are getting empty. It is also maybe because people are finding out they were lied to. The knowledge has increased and people are waking up. Only God can bring things back to order, but I don't think the world really wants this, because most of the people believe less and less in Him and this for its own lost.

CHAPTER 8

Although after my brother's departure and before I left for my return to Saskatchewan, my mom got curious again and continued to ask questions.

Tell me anyway James, how come there are weeds in Matthew or if you like it better, some lies?" "Well, the reason for someone to make this Jesus to say he's not the son of David is simply to reinforce the idea or the fact Jesus was fathered by the Spirit of God. This is an abomination according to God Himself. To understand this well you'll have to read Genesis 6 from 1 to 7. God was so mad with his sons or his angels for doing this that He wanted to destroy everything that moves on the face of the earth. It is written in there that the daughters of men gave them children. God also said his Spirit won't stay forever with men, which contradicts completely what the John of Paul said in John 14, 16, 14, 26, 15, 26, 16, 7 and 16, 13.

One thing to notice also is the fact that none others like Matthew, Mark, Luke or Peter have spoken about this Counselor. So, we have to get back to Jesus' warning in Matthew 24, 15. 'Therefore, when you see the abomination of desolation, which was spoken of through Daniel the prophet, standing in holy place, (the Bible) let the reader understand.'

The French Bible is clearer. It said; 'May the reader be careful when he reads.'

Everything is simple mom, we only have to listen to the teaching of Jesus carefully and everything becomes clear and easy to understand. It is at least for me." "You also said something about the blasphemy against the Holy Spirit." "You should know mom that all sins, what ever the ones, are against God and by the same token against the Holy Spirit also. But see, this is a diabolic machination and the only purpose is to make people believe that Paul, who came in the picture after Jesus departure is the Counsellor, the supposedly spirit of truth that supposedly Jesus was to send down when he has reached his Father in heaven. But Jesus, the true Prophet has never said such a thing, I'm sure. If he did, Matthew would have talked about it too.

It's the John of Paul who told us such a big lie to help trap the world and as far as I can tell about Christianity and my family, he succeeded it on a big scale. I hope with all of my heart that my books will help to open the eyes of a few. But we can't blame God for the wickedness of men and the wickedness and the craftiness of the devil.

God, the Father did a lot for us to know the truth and He went as far as to rise up a prophet among the brothers of Israel, the descendants of King David. The devil only had to lie by saying the opposite of Jesus' teaching and billions of people fell in his trap. It is hard to understand and all this is very sad.

Although, I still have to alert all the nations of the world about this diabolic machination and you can be sure the devil will be opposing me and my books. When I talk about the devil this mean also all of his institutions and they are rich and powerful and I am only a poor man. But God is with me and this is why I don't fear despite all the risks and I will continue until I'm done.

One pastor of a Christian church told me once that my books will go no where. We'll see what kind of prophet he is or was. He was quite old then and he might have just met his judgement already, because this was like seventeen years ago. He told me once that me and him were on the same path; something I believed at the time, but I had to change my mind since. I told me then that if he had the choice, he would be an apostle like Paul. I said right away that we would be like water is to fire to each other, because I would want to be like Peter to whom Jesus gave the keys of the kingdom of heaven and on the faith of whom Jesus built his church. A church based on a good foundation, the truth that comes from God and not like Paul's churches that are deceiving from one end to the other of its existence and it's basically made to collect money, then a business.

The worse is that Paul used the word of God, the truth to do it by manipulating it with all kind of diabolic deviations, just like the devil did it in the Garden of Eden with Adam and Eve."

"Can you explain this to me in an easier way?" "It is not always easy, but I will try to do it for you.

What happened when God told Adam and Eve they will certainly die if they disobey? The devil told Adam and Eve the opposite that they won't die, they will become like God, their eyes will open and they will know good and evil. Adam and Eve disobeyed and they didn't die physically, but they died spiritually; which the devil has forbidden telling them about it. He is crafty the enemy. It is sad to say, but the devil has almost succeeded to make God looks like a liar, because Adam and Eve didn't die right away like the devil mentioned it.

As you can see mom; we have an obvious example of the way the devil operates. God says one thing and the devil says the opposite. The only way we can see these things is by listening to Jesus and paying good attention when we read.

Now, God who is goodness and has patience, mercy almost without limits never quitted sending us prophets to warn us about the consequences for our disobedience and to teach us what we can do to be pleasing to Him. Despite being stiff-necked people and our tendency to listen to his enemy; God continues sending to us some prophets and disciples to tell us the truth and make his will known to us, though even in my family there are some who don't want to hear about it.

It is through dreams, visions and thoughts that God let me know what He wants from me and He wouldn't have done this if I didn't love Him with all my heart, my soul and my mind. With his infinite goodness He offered me this gigantic challenge to warn all the nations about the coming end to this world the way it is. In fact, we are almost there and the world, as Jesus said it continues to have fun like it was at the time of Noah. We can read it in Matthew 24, 38-39. 'For in the days before the flood, people were eating and drinking, marrying and giving in marriage, up to the day Noah entered the ark; and they knew nothing about what would happen until the flood came and took them all away. That is how it will be at the coming of the Son of Man.'

Not to forget that at the time of Noah, before the flood, God managed to put his children, the ones who loved Him to safety to protect them from the disaster. They must have had to smell the dropping of the animals for a year, but they were safe and alive.

The coming of the Son of Man will be the time of the judgement, in case someone doesn't know what this means. Jesus told us the tree that doesn't bear any good fruits will be cut and thrown into the fire. It is also written in Matthew 7, 19.

God asked men and women to be fruitful, to multiply and to fill up the earth. It is written in Genesis 1, 28 and in Genesis 9, 1. God also said it was not good for a man to be alone and He gave him a woman called Eve and said she was a suitable partner for him. This is in Genesis 2, 18.

One more time the crafty one came to say the opposite of what God had said and you can read it in 1 Corinthians 7, 1. 'For the matters you wrote about: it is good for a man not to marry.'

In other Bibles it is written: 'Not to touch a woman.' As if the woman was a dirty thing. Seeing what he wrote, I guess for Paul she is. From there began the largest homosexuals and pedophiles club ever created; which is no doubt pleasing the devil, but certainly not pleasing the Creator who made man to his image, which means creators, capable to multiply. See Genesis 1, 27.

Jesus said the tree that bears no fruit will be cut and thrown into the fire. It is up to everyone to straighten up and to remember that God is infinitely good, extremely patient and mainly very merciful, but don't mock Him, because that according to Jesus, He doesn't like hypocrisy, something you can read all over Matthew 23. Remember too that if Jesus asked us to forgive up to 490 times in a day someone who has sin against us and has repented, how many times do you think God can forgive you? See Matthew 18, 21-22. 'Then Peter came to Jesus and asked, "Lord, how many times should I forgive my brother when he sins against me? Up to seven times?" Jesus answered, "I tell you, not seven times, but seventy times seven."'

So, don't expect to be forgiven if you don't forgive, especially your brother. Everyone is Jesus' brother and mine, the one who does the will of the Father who is in heaven.

I composed another song that I like particularly, another one that was given to me from the Lord. I called it:

The Last Warning

Listen to this one great news sent to you today
To me it's the greatest; the Lord is in his way
He has made the universe, the earth and heavens
And all that you can see has been made by his hands.
"Many times I have showed you the mighty power
I have flooded the earth, but I have saved Noah.
When Abram the good man has pleaded for his friends
They got out of the towns, Sodom and Gomorrah.

Do you remember Joseph I sent to exile?
He was sold by his brothers, he was put in jail.
He was to save my people from the starvation
Of a deadly famine seven years duration.
And what to say of Moses drew out of water
To guide you to the crises and a lot of danger?
I told him all I wanted as for you to know.
He carried all my commands down to you below.

The wisdom of Solomon, the strength of Samson
Cannot just save your soul from the lake of fire.
Only Jesus the saviour with his compassion
Left his beautiful home they took him for ransom.
I sent you my loved son his life he sacrificed
He has done nothing wrong, yet he has paid the price
Now if you are telling Me this is not for you.
Just one more thing to say; I've done all I can do.

Now you are out of time and I am out of blood
Too many of my children have died for their God.

Many of Jesus good friends and his apostles
And so many others died as his disciples.
Now it is time to crown my own beloved son.
He's going back to run everything I have done
Will you be lost forever or will you be saved?
This is what you should know before you hit the grave."

Listen to this one great news sent to you today
To me it's the greatest; the Lord is in his way
He has made the universe, the earth and heavens
And all that you can see has been made by his hands.
Yes all that you can see has been made by his hands.

People can say all they want to say, such song couldn't be composed by someone who is coming from evil, even if I was accused of it, but don't you worry; I don't leave those demons disturb me anymore.

I follow Jesus, I follow God, I follow both of them step by step and I say this in our language so there is no confusion. I don't pretend to be one or the other, although I am one with both of them." "You're going to stop this nonsense right away; what you're saying here is inconceivable." "Why is this mom?" "Because we can't make one with God; we are not good enough for that." "It is though Jesus' prayer that we become one with him and with God and if it is Jesus' prayer I can't see why it wouldn't happen. See John 17, 21. 'That all of them (Jesus' disciples) may be one, Father, just as you are in me and I am in You. May they also be in us so that the world may believe that You have sent me.'"

"This is incredible James, are you sure you read this right?" "There are very strange things in the gospel of this John mom, I agree.

Although, as I was reading this story, this supposedly Jesus' prayer, I found something very strange and I think this Jesus kind of contradicts himself from John 17, 11 and John 17, 16.

John 17, 11. 'But they (Jesus' apostles) are still in the world.'

John 17, 16. 'They (Jesus' apostles) are not of the world.'

I remember mom that you were saying we weren't of the world when we were playing and making a lot of noise." "It is true that sometimes you were out of this world." "What do you think we were then?" "I think you were little demons." "Maybe you just solved a mystery of the Bible mom.

And as you will also find in the Bible, most of the contradictions from the enemy are about the Law of God. I can assure you that they are there in big numbers.

Fist of all, it's God Himself who told us about his Law and his commandments and it is pretty hard to be more specific.

It is very important for everyone to always remember the verse 31, 36 of Jeremiah. 'Only if these decrees vanish from my sight declares the Lord, will the descendants of Israel ever cease to be a nation before me.'

This verse is most likely one of the main reasons why so many nations on the earth tried to eliminate the nation of Israel and are still trying to this day. Israel is still being attacked from different nations nowadays, but it was established by God and has solid foundations. Israel's enemies who are also God's enemies would like to see Israel disappear the same way they tried to make the Law of God disappear. The fact God said the Law will never disappear and the fact some of God's enemies said the Law does no longer exist are definitely related. The devil would love to demonstrate that God made a mistake and that He failed his word, but Israel still exists and so is the Law of God, but this is not because the devil and his angels didn't try. Rome that is the base of your dear Catholic Church did everything in its power to eliminate Israel from the years 67 to 73 A.D. When Hitler and his armies tried to eliminate the Jews, the nation of Israel from 1939 to 1945, backed by Rome, there was more then the hatred of the Jews involved, this was a gigantic effort to make the Law of God disappeared like Paul tried so hard to do. What I just said or written, I never read it anywhere and I never heard of it either. This is another proof that God is speaking to me.

Then God who put his words in the mouth of Jesus, a Prophet like Moses that God raised from the brothers of Israel; saying he would do everything God's commands him, said that not the smallest letter, not the least stroke of a pen will disappear from the Law for as long as the earth and heaven exist. You can read both stories in Deuteronomy 18, 18 and in Matthew 5, 17-18.

It won't surprise me if the devil tries next to make the earth and heaven disappear with the purpose to prove that God is not quite right. This is what he's been doing from the beginning.

One more time the devil showed up to contradict God again and this times and times again.

I already talked about Ephesians 2, 15, where Paul said that Jesus abolished the Law with its commandments and regulations by dying on the cross. Of course this doesn't make sense at all. I will expose a few passages to prove my point.

I think the one message from Paul that seduced the world the most is written in Romans 6, 14. 'For sin shall not be master over you, for you are not under the law but under grace.'

But they also say they all have sins, what a grace! I think Jesus would agree with me on this one too. See

Matthew 7, 23. 'Then I will tell them plainly, 'I never knew you. Away from me, evildoers!''

See, there is a need to be a law to be punished by the law, but if there is no law; then we can't break it. No one can break a law that doesn't exist. According to the devil; if there is no law, there is no sin. Although you'll be doing much better to believe and to listen to Jesus who said the law will never disappear.

Another contradiction about the Law of God that I think seduced a lot of people is in Romans 7, 6. 'But now, by dying to what once bound us, we have been released from the law so that we serve in the new way of the Spirit, and not in the old way of the written code.'

See also Galatians 3, 24-25. 'So the law was put in charge to lead us to Christ that we might be justified by faith. Now that faith has come, we are no longer under the supervision of the law.'

I hope that one day I'll have the time to count all the verses where the word of God and the messages of Jesus are contradicted by Paul and company about the Law of God.

There are also a lot of contradictions concerning the circumcision and this by the same author, which is in fact an everlasting covenant between God and his children, just like the rainbow that we can see now and then.

When Jesus in Matthew 24, 15 talked about the abomination that causes desolation in the holy place, here is another one and it is the most obvious I think about the circumcision and it is written in Galatians 5, 2. 'Behold I, Paul say to you that if you receive circumcision, Christ will be of no benefit to you.'

No matter how hard we try not to talk bad about someone; what is above is completely unacceptable, at least by a Jesus' disciple who loves to do the will of God and I don't take it.

There is another one that is quite a bit out of the ordinary. See Galatians 5, 12. 'As for those agitators, (the circumcision group) I wish they would go the whole way and emasculate themselves.'

As you too can see for yourselves; the will of Paul is completely opposite to the will of God and his teaching is completely opposite to the teaching of Jesus. And of course, all the Christians churches are from Paul and this would explain why their teaching is from Paul too and not the teaching of Jesus, which is from God. This is also the reason why Christians are so astonished when they hear the truth; this is something they are not used to.

It is most likely because Paul used the word of God to mislead; exactly the same way the serpent, the devil used the word of God in the Garden of Eden to mislead Adam and Eve. This seems contradictory, but it is actually very crafty. He also, as a crafty man that he is put his venom among Jesus' disciples and Jesus' apostles. This is one thing very well explained in the parable of the weeds by Jesus in Matthew 13, 13-43.

Here in Galatians 5, 14 is a very distinctive example of what I'm saying and I like you to compare it with a similar story in Matthew 22, 36-40. Just a few very important details make a great difference.

Galatians 5, 14. 'The entire law is summed up in a single command: "Love your neighbour as yourself."'

As you'll see, these words are only one part of the Jesus' important messages, but in Paul's statement, the most important is not there.

Take a look now at the complete messages from Jesus concerning the Law of God and the commandments. See Matthew 22, 36-40. '"Teacher, which is the greatest commandment in the Law?" Jesus replied: "'Love the Lord your God with all your heart and with all your soul and with all your mind.' This is the first and the greatest commandment. And the second is like it: 'Love your neighbour as yourself.' All the Law and the Prophets hang on these two commandments.'"

Jesus didn't say the Law was summed up and he didn't say either this was in one command, but that the whole Law and the prophets hang on these two commandments, which is a big difference. Jesus said we have to love God with all our strength, something Paul couldn't say and couldn't do.

I would like now to bring you back to a similar situation at the beginning of the Bible in Genesis 2, 17 and Genesis 3, 4-5. You will see that Paul and the serpent, the craftiest of all the animals on earth have both strangely acted in a very similar way.

God said; Genesis 2, 17. 'But you must not eat from the tree of the knowledge of good and evil, for when you eat it you will surely die.'

The human beings were created to live almost eternally. I don't think it was as long as the angels, because angels know the difference between good and evil.

See now Genesis 3, 4-5. ' "You will not surely die," the serpent said to the woman. "For God knows that when you eat of it your eyes will be opened, and you will be like God, knowing good and evil."'

Did you recognize the craftiness that is the same or at least very similar than Paul's way. Did you see that the serpent just like Paul used the word of God to mislead? I would like now for you to meditate on what Paul wrote in 2 Corinthians 12, 16. 'Be that as it may, I have not been a burden to you. Yet, crafty fellow that I am, I caught you by trickery!'

We have to remember as well the Jesus' instructions to his apostles and disciples. They don't have to worry about their living, because the people they instruct should take care of that. See Matthew 10, 9-10. 'Do not take any gold or silver or copper in your belts; take no bag for the journey, or extra tunic, or sandals or a staff for the worker is worth his keep.'

I'm afraid that today I would starve to death if I rely on people I try to instruct about the truth, the word of God to feed me.

The trick for Paul was to say to his disciples; 'See, I don't take anything from you to teach you the lies.'

Although we don't have to lift our eyes very high to see that Paul's followers paid a lot more than staff, shoes and food to their leaders who mislead them and continue to do so. We only have to look at the St. Peter's Basilica and at the Vatican City, at the Vatican wine cavern to understand they got a lot more than necessary. That goes too to all of Paul's Christian churches that are imitating the Church of Rome and disguised themselves a bit more as angel of light to better trap their victims. Their leaders are called, 'Pastors,' instead of, 'Fathers,' but the bottom line is, it means the same thing.

As I remember the sermons that I heard when I was still going to the Baptist Evangelic Church, the pastor was talking about Paul and his achievements for about a half hour and he was finishing by saying; This is the favour I'm asking You Father in the name of your Son Jesus. This was approximately 99 % about Paul and barely 1 % about God and Jesus to finish with. No wonder why the vast majority of Christians knows the teaching of Paul and ignore the teaching of Jesus. And to top it all; the whole congregation was in a mood of applause for their pastor who seduced them with a multitude of lies and contradictions. Paul said: 'Be my imitators.'

I remember among others the sermon about the Paul's rapture, which can't be more opposed to Jesus' parable of the weeds. I was under the impression the whole congregation was ready to fly up in the air and go join Paul and the dead in Christ on the clouds and to be with their lord for the eternity. Something the members of this congregation don't seem to know or to understand is that the ones who are going to be taken away at the end time are the weeds, the wicked, the ones who say; 'We all have sins.' Jesus said it.

To understand this right we have to be very careful when we read Matthew 13, 41-43 and Matthew 24, 38-39.

Let's see first the Paul's rapture that is written in 1 Thessalonians 4, 16-17. 'The dead in Christ will rise first. After that, we (Paul and his followers) who are still alive will be caught up together with them (the dead in Christ) in the clouds to meet the lord in the air. And so we will be with the lord forever.'

I hope for their own good they won't have fear of the heights.

Now, according to Jesus, the true Prophet of God and what he said in Matthew 13, 41-43 and here it is. 'The Son of Man (means a prophet, not God) will send out his angels, and they will weed out of his Kingdom (means, on earth) everything that causes sin and all who do evil. (The sinners) They will throw them into the fiery furnace, where there will be weeping and gnashing of teeth. Then the righteous (none sinners) will shine like the sun in the kingdom of their Father. He who has ears, let him hear.'

Here is another message from Jesus on the same subject in Matthew 24, 37. 'As it was at the time of Noah, so it will be at the coming of the Son of Man.'

Do you really know the story of Noah and the flood? Well yes, the ones who all had sins were taken away. They didn't get caught on the clouds, but they were all swallowed by the waters, by the flood, while the righteous were put to safety. This is the way God operates and you can be sure that He'll do it again. Anyway, the ones who were taken away were the wicked, the sinners. So I suggest that you listen to Jesus of Nazareth, the one who tells us the truth. This way you'll have a chance to live happily an eternal life, word of God, the true One.

Now, I understand very well that many of you who are reading this book of mine, that you didn't know that you were mislead this way by God's enemies, but between you and me; this shouldn't be the case anymore, should it?

On the other hand, if you change camp to join the Jesus' disciples, don't you go throw yourselves in the mouth of the wolves unnecessarily. This is also a good warning that was given to us by Jesus.

None of the Jesus' disciples, at least in everything that I have read, mentioned the words; 'Bishop, archbishop, cardinal, pope, priest or deacon. This is kind of a proof one more time that the Christians churches are invented by Paul, which is in my opinion the biggest trap and the biggest scandal of all times in the human race.

But Jesus came to set us free, to free us from the slavery that religions impose and free us from sinning. According to all Jesus' messages, he sure didn't want us to be slaves of religions. I have a small hope that the new law that was voted to protect the denouncers will succeed in protecting me from one, if not the most powerful institution in the world, Christianity, but I have my doubts, because it is basically set up everywhere in the world. Israel, one of the nicest countries in the world, the country of the people of God will probably be the only place for me as a shelter, besides God of course. One thing is sure, I will not go hide at my brother's place, because Jesus warned me already.

Our Prime Minister has most likely received the warning too, because he holds firm and steady for Israel and against the Palestine and the rest of the world.

Jesus said the scandals are necessary and I can understand why, but I believe the biggest scandal of all times is the religious system, Christianity. I even thing it is the beast of the end time. Just to think they have called the devil: 'saint,' and all their descendants, the popes: 'holy father.' We don't have to look any farther to know this is totally antichrist. Take a look again to see what Jesus said in Matthew 23 from 1 to 12 and you will realize that neither Jesus nor God wanted this diabolic hierarchy.

Now, if you want to know who invented Christianity and all of its churches, you only have to read Philippians 1, 1, 1 Timothy 2 from 8 to 12 and 1 Timothy 3, 1-8.

1 Timothy 2, 8. 'I (Paul) want men everywhere to lift up holy hands in prayer, without anger or disputing.'

This looks as it could be good, but this is also antichrist, because Jesus, the Christ said to go in your room to pray. See Matthew 6, 5-6.

Again here Jesus is contradicted by Paul. And I continue. 1 Timothy 2, 9-12. 'I (Paul) want women to dress modestly, with decency and propriety, not with braided hair or gold or pearls or expensive clothes, but with good deeds, appropriate for women who profess to worship God. A woman should learn in quietness and full submission. (Anyone can tell that this has changed a little) I don't permit a woman to teach or to have authority over a man; she must be silent.'

Be pretty and quiet. Did you get this, women? This too has changed a little.

See now 1 Timothy 3, 8. 'Deacons likewise, are to be men worthy of respect, sincere, not indulging in much wine, and not pursuing dishonest gain.'

Philippians 1, 1. 'Paul and Timothy, servants of Christ Jesus, to all the saints in Christ Jesus at Philippi, together with the overseers and deacons.'

Paul talked about all the saints, but Jesus said that only One is good; this is not the same language, not the same teaching at all. In all of Jesus messages you have never heard him talked about the instructions Paul talked about and never Jesus mentioned the hierarchy of the Christian churches. Take a look in Matthew 10, 1-42 for the mission of the Jesus' disciples and Jesus' instructions to them. There is no overseer (bishop) and no deacon. Jesus said his disciples were all equal, none above the others.

Do you have enough? I hope you have enough of this to turn to God and to turn to Jesus' teaching instead of Paul's. But if this is not enough for you; I can still show you a lot of these contradictions and lies from Paul and company.

Here are the names of the twelve apostles according to Matthew in the New Testament that Jesus spent three years instructing. Matthew 10, 2-5. 'These are the names of the twelve apostles; first, Simon (who is called Peter) and his brother Andrew; James son of Zebedee, and his brother John; Philip and Bartholomew; Tomas and Matthew the tax collector; James son of Alphaeus, and Thaddaeus; Simon the Zealot and Judas Iscariot, who betrayed him. These twelve Jesus sent out with the following instructions.'

Thanks to God we have Matthew. All we have from Andrew, Philip, Bartholomew, the second James, Thaddaeus and the second Simon the Zealot are as far as I know their names. We have the incredulity of Thomas and yet, this is not mentioned anywhere else than in John and I have good reasons to doubt it, but I'll be back to it later. We have the death of the first

James, killed by Herod, who was executing the Jesus' disciples once Paul presumably joined the apostles. We have of course the story of Judas. We don't have much about Peter and I suspect greatly it is because he was contradicting Paul and the Romans. See Acts 21, 21.

We don't have much from the John, Jesus' apostle, although him, Peter and James were practically following Jesus together just about everywhere. It was these three who were with Jesus when the transfiguration occurred, but strangely the John of the gospel of John didn't talk about it and yet, this must have been an event out of the ordinary.'

One of my sisters told me one day that she doesn't listen to Peter, John and James when I tried to inform her about some contradictions in the Bible. This is a French expression that means: 'She doesn't listen to everybody. It is just too bad she didn't give herself a chance to know the truth. I can't even blame her, because billions of others received this brainwashing that is almost irremediable.

When came the night, my nephew who was also visiting at my mom started questioning me about the messages of the Bible. He is already done with his high school and he is about to begin higher studies. He started reading out loud in 1 Corinthians as we both had a Bible in hands and I was following as he read. It was unbelievable to see how he could read this much without knowing and understanding what he was reading. So I interrupted him many times to bring him to realize and to reflect on what he just read. Then once he heard the explanation he seemed to understand. All this to say I believe that most people do the same; reading the Bible without understanding it too much and this is why so many people got fooled by the religious leaders. I most likely did the same thing; I mean read the Bible for years without understanding too much of it and this until God came to wake me up about the presence of the antichrist in this precious book, the abomination that causes desolation in the holy place.

Ho I had detected a few contradictions that I mentioned to a priest, who was a leader of the Bible's studies. He told me then that I was right, but I had to give the church a chance that it was young. I told him then the Catholic Church was almost two thousand years old and with all of its members doesn't understand what a young man understands. I was only in my early twenties then.

So I had to repeat it to my young nephew what Jesus had said in Matthew 24, 15. 'May the reader be careful when he reads! I think many people do the same thing when they pray. They keep babbling the same things over and over again without really meaning what they say. This is also a thing Jesus warned us not to do. See Matthew 6, 7. 'When you pray, do not keep on babbling like pagans, for they think they will be heard because of their many words.'

We all know too that a multitude of people are praying other than God; which must be very frustrating to Him, because He said Himself being a jealous God. And Jesus said to give to God what belongs to God. See Matthew 22, 21.

Jesus told us who to pray, where, how and when to pray. See Matthew 6, 6 to Matthew 6, 13.

I asked God once to show me what I could do for Him and I chose the Psalm 104, 33-34 when I got baptized. 'I will sing to the Lord all my life: I will sing praises to my God as long as I live. May my meditation be pleasing to Him, as I rejoice in the Lord.'

I kept my word and so did He. He gave me a good twenty hymns that I keep singing practically every day, not all of them every day, but a few of them every day. I also work by writing in my books to make his will known to others, so people can see the truth, which is Jesus' last wish before his trip to heaven. See Matthew 28, 19-20.

Jesus also said in this last verse that he is with us until the end of the world. I just happen to know that we are getting very close to the end of this world as we know it today and I also know that the word of God is also with us, just as Jesus said it. But the truth is not well known to people. For example, my old mother of ninety years old and she was a religious person all of her life; she was a catholic for many years, she was also a Baptist evangelic for many years and she knows very little of the truth. And believe me, she's not alone.

It is though not just a question of will, but also a question of luck. Having the luck to know the truth is not a thing accessible to everybody like many of the ones who will read my book will have the opportunity to notice. This is why I'm asking everyone who has the luck to read it to give this chance to others as well. If this happens to be your case; I suggest you lend it instead of giving it; so it doesn't end up on a shelf collecting dust and not helping anyone anymore. By getting it back; this is giving you the chance to lend it to someone else who might just enjoy receiving the truth. You can also refer this book to others; which will be for you a good deed in bringing an important contribution in Jesus' mission that is to alert all the nations. Jesus who said all will know the truth before the end, see Matthew 24, 14. 'And this gospel of the kingdom of heaven will be preached in the whole world as a testimony to all nations, and then the end will come.'

If you are on Jesus' side; you have no reason to fear the end of the world, because if you read carefully the word of God, Jesus' message about it, you will shine like the sun in the kingdom of our Father. If you allow me to give you a good advice, I would tell you to spread the truth instead of hiding it like the leaders of these Christian churches do it. At least if you don't want to bring the wrath of God against yourselves. See Matthew 5, 19. 'Anyone who breaks one of the least of these commandments and teaches others to do the same will be called least in the kingdom of heaven, but whoever practices and teaches these commands will be called great in the kingdom of heaven.'

See one more time Romans 1, 18. 'The wrath of God is being revealed from heaven against all the godlessness and wickedness of men who suppress the truth by wickedness.'

I know I am sometimes repeating myself, but there is some truth that can't be repeated too often, because your salvation depends on it. I wouldn't want to be in the shoes of Paul's churches' leaders who have been suppressing the truth for many years. They're suppressing the truth because they are not in a hurry the get to their end.

I talked earlier about Thomas that we don't have much of. What is very sad is that what we have I believe is nothing but a lie. Read carefully John 20, 17. 'Jesus said, "Do not hold on to me, for I have not yet returned to the Father. Go instead to my brothers and tell them, 'I am returning to my Father and your Father, to my God and your God.'

Read now carefully what is in John 20, 27-29. 'Then Jesus said to Thomas, "Put your finger here; see my hands. Reach out your hand and put it into my side. Stop doubting and believe." Thomas said to him, "My Lord and my God." Then Jesus told him, "Because you have seen me, you have believed; blessed are those who have not seen and yet have believed."'

Then the message was launched that you have to believe blindly. This is what most of the Christians have been doing almost forever, to believe anyone and anything.

There is another message a little strange dissimulated in the Thomas' story. You try to find out what it is and I'll come back later on in this page to tell you what I found. I'm asking you to play the game with me simply because I want you to start decoding the Scriptures. Read carefully from John 20, 16 to John 20, 29, just to see if you're going to see what I saw.

We all know that Jesus is the light of the world and the light travels at 186000 miles in one second. Maybe the Jesus of the Thomas' story in this gospel of John had the time to go see his Father in heaven after talking to Mary in John 20, 16-17, telling her not to touch him and come back in time to tell Thomas in John 20, 27 to touch him so he can believe in him.

If you are very careful by reading the gospel of John; you too will find other things that I can say are at least very strange. But before I go any farther I want to tell you now what I found very strange in the gospel of John from verses 20, 16 to John 20, 29. It is that a woman by the name of Mary Magdalene, known to be one of Jesus' close friends and maybe one of his disciples too couldn't touch Jesus, not even his hand, while a man by the name of Thomas could do it. All of this according to this story at the request of this same Jesus.

It is true that a certain apostle said; "It is not good for a man to touch a woman." Who was this again? Ho yes, this is Paul in 1 Corinthians 7, 1, the master of this John.

I don't know what you think about this, but for myself, I find way more enjoyable to be touch by a woman than by a man, even if it's only the hand.

But this doesn't stop here. You too will see, at least I hope so, that there are a lot of other things, other stories that show the tendency of this John towards people of the same sex. Don't be fooled though, because the John mentioned here is not the John apostle of the true Jesus.

I will start with John 13, 4. This is the story where Jesus apparently got undressed completely to wash the feet of his apostles. It is for sure a story that is completely unlikely. This is also a story that is not mentioned anywhere else. I am also sure that if this situation really occurred; Matthew too would have talked about it, but he didn't. That Jesus, the true one, the Son of Man, who is the Son of God and whom many say he's God became man, would have got completely undressed before his apostles when we know that Canaan was cursed and reduced to slavery, because his father saw the nakedness of his father Noah? Think about it for a minute, would you? Jesus was humble, yes, but he was not a pervert.

Then we can see that the camouflage is already started. See John 13, 4. 'He (Jesus) riseth from supper, and laid aside his garments, (Jesus only had two pieces of clothing) and took a towel and girded himself.'

I read in a newer Bible in John 13, 4 that Jesus took off his outer garment instead of his garments. Someone like me mentioned it before and someone else understood that this has no sense at all. So they changed; his garments in John 13, 4 for his outer garments, but they were too stupid to dress him in John 13, 12. 'When he had finished washing their feet, he put his clothes on and returned to his place.'

They are very bright these church people, but they are not as crafty as their master Paul was.

Then we have the disciple that Jesus loved, see John 21, 7. 'Then the disciple whom Jesus loved said to Peter,

"It is the Lord!" As soon as Simon Peter heard him say, "It is the Lord," he girt his fisher's coat unto him, for he was naked and did cast himself into the sea.'

To put so many abominations in the same verse, only a devilish person could do it.

See now the same story in a newer Bible. John 21, 7. 'As soon as Simon Peter heard, "It is the Lord," he wrapped his outer garment around him, for he had taken it off, and jumped into the water.'

I imagine that being completely naked before the Son of God for the most considerate of all the apostles must be embarrassing enough to jump into the sea, even if we don't know how to swim. According to Matthew 14, 30, Peter didn't know how to swim. 'But when Peter saw the wind, he was afraid and, beginning to sink, cried out, "Lord, save me."'

Then, this John, this disciple that supposedly Jesus loved more than the others was the only one to recognize Jesus on the sea shore. This is very strange, because according to the same author of this gospel of John, not very long before the shore story, Jesus appeared to all of them. It couldn't have been long, because Jesus stayed with his apostles only forty days after his resurrection. See John 20, 26. 'A week later Jesus' disciples were in the house again, and Thomas was with them. Though the doors were locked, Jesus came and stood among them and said.'

Then Jesus who has never pretended to be the father of anyone, contrary to Paul, even when he was talking to children or about children, would have called the men on the shore, "Children." See John 21, 5. 'Then Jesus saith unto them, Children, have ye any meat? They answered him, no.'

Again in the newer and revised Bibles it is a bit different. They came up with, 'Friends,' instead of, 'Children.'

Then they took so many fish that all of these men on the boat couldn't pull the net in. See John 21, 6. 'They were unable to haul the net in because of the large number of fish.'

But they could pull it to shore without Peter who had thrown himself into the see. We don't know how Peter could make it to shore, but according to the story, he made it anyway.

Then Peter, John 21, 11 climbed aboard and dragged the net ashore by himself, because the others had landed, see John 21, 9.

Then Jesus, John 21, 13, came near the fire where he was already and took the bread and gave it to them and he did the same with the fish.

And for the first time of the Bible' history, neither this Jesus nor the disciples gave grace to God for the bread and the fish, the food they all got to eat basically by miracle.

CHAPTER 9

It is a bit by miracle also that I can still work in my books today, because I was forced by the events to get out of the province of Quebec in 1982. I have had a lot of threats following a business bankruptcy and even our family tent trailer was stolen in front of our house in the early hours of a morning and my young children could have been sleeping in it. The thief, a creditor took it while it was secured with a padlock and for this reason he couldn't secure it to his vehicle. So he lost it on his way home, at about three miles farther and the trailer was a total lost. Later on that day I received a phone call from his lawyer asking me how much I wanted for this trailer. So this creditor had to buy this tent trailer that he couldn't enjoy more than a few minutes and he had to erase my debt at the same time to avoid being accused of stealing with premeditation. I would say he found a way to get himself in trouble.

There were many other threats of this kind and this is what incited me to move out of my province thinking my children would be a lot safer this way. It is good to fight for justice, but it is not nice to put your family at risk. I asked for help in those days, but I didn't obtain it. I was told instead there was nothing they could do about it for me. Then I packed a few things of mine and I moved out of Quebec with the $600.00 I got from welfare. This wasn't quite enough money to make it directly to Calgary where I was heading. I was maybe at around twenty miles before my destination when I ran out of gas and out of money. I'm not the type of men to beg for help, but sometime in a life time a person has no choice. But as I was turning around on foot in a parking lot of a shopping mall; someone asked me for a boost and I explained to him my situation and telling him that I needed something like $5.00 to make it to Calgary where one of my ex employee was expecting me, but I would have given him the boost for free anyway.

I contacted this ex employee before my departure who was working for a very big construction company and they were building some high rises and they were finishing one and about to begin another one. He told me that for a carpenter like me there was a lot of work. But when we go from one trouble to another we can expect anything, can't we? The economic depression of 1982 didn't hurt only the town of Trois-Rivières in the East, but also the West of the country. I found out at my arrival the company I was to work for filed for bankruptcy as well. This was the end of September, the normal time of lay off.

So I had to baby-sit three children to make a living in my first winter in foreign ground. Just before this depression Calgary and Trois-Rivières were the two towns the most booming in Canada before that economic crash. In 1983 I could buy a duplex with a dollar down and the payments would have been less than my rent in the same building, only the interests at the bank were at 27 %.

Although, it was not the economic conditions that hurt me the most, but most likely the plot against me by my client, the bank manager and my lawyer of the time.

To take a French expression from Quebec, I was loyally screwed.

On the other hand, I don't complain, because it was most likely because God wanted to get me out of the province of Quebec, but in those days I was not thinking the way I do now. I was putting up with my misfortune without understanding what happened to me. I told a lady friend once that it was because God loves me He was putting me to test. She responded by saying He should love me a little less and reduce my burden. She was a money grabber, something I never was.

It is true that until God reveals his plan to us everything seems to be mysterious.

I lived through highs and lows in the eight years I was living in Calgary, but I had good times there also. I wouldn't want to spend too much time complaining about my misfortunes like Paul did. I don't want to be preaching James Prince in this book of mine, but the Jesus' messages, which is my priority.

The circumstances that made me get out of Alberta in 1990 are quite different, but they were just as efficient. A heck of a good thing I had my best friends with me. It is a bit sad to say, but my dogs gave me a lot more joy than anyone did. Some people would blame me for feeding animals instead of people, but without them I wouldn't have wanted to continue.

You know that dog, which, if you read backward gives you god. I am the master of my dogs and God is my Master. I know too that it is by the will of God if I have something to eat every day and a roof over my head. I am the master of my dogs and yet I'm the one who feed them that clean them and supply them with a shelter. In the ordinary course it is the jack who serves the king, isn't it? The difference between my dogs and the world is that my dogs adore me. No one can contest this fact.

Did you ever read Christian backwardly? This gives you: 'An ti christ.' Amazing isn't it? The worse is that I succeeded to prove it with the messages of Jesus in Matthew. I also discovered the name of the beast since; the name that is associated with the number six, six, six. I'm not ready yet to disclose it to the world, but this will come soon. Just try to think about how this beast will react when it finds out someone discovered it. The one who created this beast challenged the world to discover it almost two thousand years ago. I will only tell you for now that the word Christian in French, which is Chrétien got me on its trace. You can see the challenge launched by the author of this beast himself in Revelation 13, 18. 'Here is wisdom. Let him who has understanding calculate the number of the beast, for the number is that of a man, and his number is six hundred and sixty-six.' This is a number of a man.

The least one can say is this guy was quite arrogant to challenge the world; someone to be wise enough to find this number. But if he knew the number of the beast, this also means he knew his name. A Jesus' disciple wouldn't have challenged the world like this author did it, but he would have told the world who this beast is and warned us about its diabolic presence. Millions and millions have looked for this name and the beast is only waiting for anyone to show up with the answer to eliminate the wise guy. He is crafty the enemy even if he is the worst beast, the devil.

Let me give you a few clues that you no doubt most likely already know without realizing it. We already know, because Jesus told us that the devil is a murderer from the beginning, don't we? Jesus told us too the devil is a liar and the father of lies. We also know that the devil is an outlaw and is against everything coming from God, including the circumcision. This should be enough in itself for you to know who he is. To know at least who the creator of the beast is, at least once you've read this book of mine.

He is well described enough too in Daniel 11, 36-37. 'The king will do as he pleases. He will exalt and magnify himself above every god and will say unheard-of things against the God of gods. He will be successful until the time of wrath is completed, for what has been determined must take place. He will show no regard for the gods of his fathers or for the one desired by women, nor will he regard any god, but he will exalt above them all.'

These last few lines resemble a lot of what is written in 2 Thessalonians 2, 3-4. 'Don't let anyone deceive you in any way, for that day will not come until the rebellion occurs and the man of lawlessness is revealed, the man doomed to destruction. He will oppose and will exalt himself over everything that is called or is worshipped, so that he sets himself in God's temple, proclaiming himself to be God.'

This is what Paul, the man of lawlessness did and he is the one I'm revealing to the world with my writing, with my books. He is the one who set himself in the heart of millions of Christians, including many members of my own family.

This reminds me of Paul, Hitler, Saddam Hussein and all those alike, although I think Hitler and Saddam liked women. Putin is another one who just joined this group of arrogant people, not to say, monsters.

No one can say with a straight face that Paul care for women.

I personally think the true Revelation is in Daniel. Why I don't tell you the name of the beast at this point and time? Well, let just say that I follow my own advice to not throw myself in the mouths of the wolves, but this will come soon, most likely with one of my next books, which might just be the last one. I promise though to do it as soon as possible. I was going to say when it will be safe for me to do it, but this is impossible. I suspect though that when one member of the beast reads one of my books, the beast will know that I know the truth and his identity as well. As soon as the name of the beast is known, it will burst out with rage and try to find me immediately and don't go bet on my chances to survive. I didn't forget what happened to Jesus and to Louis Riel for telling the truth and denouncing this beast.

So I was saying that the circumstances forced me to get out of Alberta with as much convictions as the ones that forced me to get out of the province of Quebec. In another word; I didn't have too much choice and this was not because of my mistakes either. But I had to follow one of the Jesus' advices that is written in Matthew 10, 23. 'When you are persecuted in one place flee to another. I tell you the truth, you will not finish going through the towns of Israel before the Son of Man comes.'

Now, this means the Jesus' disciples didn't go through all the towns of Israel yet. So I have a long way to go yet. I mean me and my books. This also means I have to flee somewhere else when I am persecuted. This goes for all the Jesus' disciples if they want to follow Jesus' teaching in everything. Remember; 'Be shrewd as snakes and as innocent as doves.'

One thing I'm almost sure of is that if I had insisted in convincing all people of the church where I was going about all the truth that I found; I would probably be dead by now. No one can contribute in emptying the Christian churches without risking his life if he doesn't do it anonymously and this is not cowardice but it is cautiousness. I would even say this is the reason why God showed me to read and to write anonymously instead of talking to people and make them spit at my face and even make them throw stones at me or worse yet. Another thing I am sure of is that He showed me too to discover the lies and the contradictions in the Scripture of the Bible. In my first real study after the dream where He asked me to write, I found 503 of them and I find some more almost each time I open my Bible. When we have our eyes opened, we can see. It seems there are more of them in the gospel of John, just like in all the writing of Paul.

Here is another obvious example in John 19, 25-27. 'Near the cross of Jesus stood his mother, his mother's sister, Mary the wife of Clopas, and Mary Magdalene. When Jesus saw his mother there, and the disciple whom he loved standing nearby, he said to his mother, "Dear woman, here is your son," and to the disciple, "Here is your mother." From that time on, this disciple took her into his home.'

What a lie, what a pile of impure rubbish. I was going to say; 'Pure rubbish,' but when the rubbish is so disgusting, we cannot say it is pure. Let's not forget that Jesus' mother had three other children, three other sons and in those days children could take care of their parents. And more yet, if Jesus was so much broken down and unrecognizable; I doubt he had the strength, the time and could speak this long to his mother or to one of his disciples.

First of all, according to a true Jesus' disciple who told the true story of Jesus and other God's prophets said before him how this will happen; all of the Jesus' true disciples were scattered that day. So, there was no Jesus' disciple near the Jesus' cross, not even the disciple Jesus loved, this liar, I have to precise.

In Matthew we can read the exact opposite of this story of the gospel of this John. See Matthew 27, 55-56. 'Many women were there watching <u>from a distance</u>. They had followed Jesus from Galilee to care for his needs. Among them were Mary Magdalene, Mary the mother of James and Joses, and the mother of the Zebedee's sons.'

According to this version, the account of a true apostle; as you too can see; there was no Jesus' mother or a disciple that Jesus loved near the cross and believe me; if they had been there, neither one would have been able to tell anything to anyone anymore. We only have to read in Matthew 26, 69-75, the story of Peter disowning Jesus to see how much the lives of Jesus' apostles were at risk that day. It is easy to understand why.

Even Jesus told them they were all to be scattered that day and it was then that Peter told Jesus he will hold on to him to the end; something he could not do and I assure you that I couldn't do any better; because it was there and then the will of God he acted this way and I will explain this right away.

See Zechariah 13, 7. ' "Awake, O sword, against my shepherd, against the man who is close to Me!" declares the Lord Almighty. Strike the shepherd and the sheep will be scattered and I will turn my hand upon the little ones.'

I saw in another Bible instead of upon, it is written against, which is the exact opposite.

Jesus practically said the same thing. See Matthew 26, 31-33. 'Then Jesus told them, "This very night you will all fall away on account of me, for it is written: "'I will strike the shepherd, and all the sheep of the flock will be scattered. But after I have risen, I will go ahead of you into Galilee." Peter replied, "Even if all fall away on account of you, I never will."'

All means all, and coming from Jesus you can believe it and this also means that John the true apostle was scattered too and there is no way he would have come near Jesus' cross that day. So the John near the cross in the gospel of John is nothing but an impostor and a liar.

Do you see that God had a very good reason to act the way He did? If the Jesus' apostles wouldn't have been scattered that day; they would most likely all have been killed too and we would have next to nothing from Jesus' teaching. Neither Jesus nor God wanted to waste three years of Jesus' life. If Matthew would have been killed that day; he would certainly not be in the Bible the way we have him. In any case I am very happy to have him and mainly happy that we have something else than these liars of John and Paul and company. I have great thanks for Matthew, the first and the most important gospel; the one where we find most of the truth and mainly the kingdom of heaven. Matthew is the only one who talked about it.

Another story I find funny and sad at the same time in this gospel of John is the story of the wedding at Cana. See John 2, 1-11. 'On the third day a wedding took place at Cana in Galilee. Jesus' mother was there, and Jesus and his disciples had also been invited to the wedding. When the wine was gone, Jesus' mother said to him, "They have no more wine." "Dear woman, why do you involve me?" Jesus replied. "My time has not yet come." His mother said to the servants, "Do whatever he tells you." Nearby stood six stone water jars; the kind used by the Jews for the ceremonial washing, (bathtubs) each holding twenty to thirty gallons. Jesus said to the servants, "Fill the jars with water;" so they filled them to the brim. Then he told them, "Now draw some out and take it to the master of the banquet." They did so, and the master of the banquet tasted the water that had been turned into wine. He did not realize where it had come from, though the servants who had drawn the water knew. Then he called the bridegroom aside and said, "Everyone bring out the choice wine first and then the cheaper wine after the guests had too much to drink;

but you have saved the best till now." This, the first of his miraculous signs, Jesus performed at Cana in Galilee.'

My French Bible says this was Jesus' first miracle and it was done at Cana in Galilee. If this was the case, how Jesus' mother, the st Mary would have known her son Jesus could do this kind of miracles? I personally didn't know at all I could write a book before I had one done. Secondly, I never thought of it until I had a dream where Jesus asked me to write for him. I believe in it so little that I laughed at him and I argued telling him I couldn't even spell the words properly. So what I think is that, if Jesus never had made a miracle yet; he couldn't know he could and his mother even less.

This is not all. How Jesus who is gentle and humble at heart could more or less tell his mother to mind her own business in this story of water changed to wine and tell her his time has not yet come?

This is not all yet. How it is that Jesus, the Son of Man, the Son of God, whom many say he is God could have made from 120 to 180 gallons of the best wine to a group of people who was already drunk?

Well, if to make up to 180 gallons of a good, the best intoxicating wine for people of a wedding already drunk was the way for the Jesus of this gospel of John to make his disciples believing in him; I'm afraid I would have stayed fairly incredulous.

I want to believe and I even think I have lots of faith, but certainly not in these kind of ridicules stories like the water changed to wine by this John who is certainly not the John, apostle of Jesus.

Yes I believe, but I believe in the truth and this even if I was poisoned with lies and contradictions from the Christian churches. This story must have taken a lot of people in its trap, because I'm not young anymore and I have never heard anyone talked about it the way I do.

I heard a joke one time that I'll take the time to tell you anyway, because laughing is good for us too. Here it is. 'One man got stopped by a cop one day and he asked the driver if he minds to open his trunk. The man agree saying, 'There is no problem at all.'

Of course the cop discovered this man was carrying many gallons of red wine in his car. The driver tells the cop he is carrying many gallons of holy water for his church. But when the cop opened one of these bottles, he found out immediately the holy water has a strong smell of alcohol. When this cop asked the man for an explanation, the driver answered him by thanking the Lord for doing it another time.'

The cop didn't believe in this man story anymore than I believe in the John of this gospel and I think it is justified in both cases.

We were filled just like turkeys the same way the jars of this story were filled with water. Just like I was saying, it is finny and sad at the same time.

God got me out of British Columbia with circumstances even more convincing than my two first exits and maybe I became a bit more receptive to Jesus' messages. You will be able to read the whole story in another book, if I ever have the chance to publish it and it's called: The Rough Road or The Golden Path?

It is with the help of many dreams and visions that allowed me to understand before it was too late that I had to get out and this quickly. There is a good reason why Jesus asked us not to attach ourselves to the good of this world and to instead accumulate treasures in heaven.

I heard many people say they will die where they were born. It is good to be patriotic, but not to the point of giving your life for it. Our patriarchs Abraham, Isaac, Jacob, Joseph, the sons of Israel and even all the people of Israel and many more had to flee to exile to survive. Even Joseph, Jesus' biological father and Mary, Jesus' mother had to flee to Egypt to survive. Even Jesus had to flee again and again to save his life.

To me it is completely ridicules to think we must die where we were born. We are all born dirty, but someone cleans us as soon as possible. I was born in the straw bed of my mother, but I travelled a very long way since. This doesn't mean a thing where I will die; either it is in a bed that belonged to my mom or not. I think these people are definitely too superstitious and they should, for their own good, put their faith in God instead.

Did you ever think of how many sins people are committing directly because of their religion? You should know by now that Jesus did enormously to pull the world away from the slavery of religions to lead it towards God, the Father. You should know too that the devil did the exact opposite and did everything possible to keep people under the slavery of religions. Millions of murders were committed directly caused by religions and among them are the murders of Jesus and of Louis Riel, the apostle Peter, James and many, many Jesus' disciples and this in every century. The last would war was nothing else than a war of religions. It was then a war from Catholics against Judaism. In fact, this is a war that has been lasting since the beginning between good and evil, between God and the devil.

The atheists who say God doesn't exist and neither the devil have to be absolutely blind not to see that good and evil exist, because we have both of them before are own eyes every day of our life. I even think a two years old child could prove it to us. The whole world is an enormous galley. Everything that happens in the court houses proves this too. Just about everything that happens in the school yards proves this too. Just try to visualize a single movie or a TV show without seeing good and evil. There is a battle between good and evil practically in every family in the world and some stupid people dare say this doesn't exist. What do they need, frankly?

There is a story in the Bible that I found quite funny and it is in Luke 16, 19-31. 'There was a rich man who was dressed in purple and fine linen and lived in luxury every day. At his gate was laid a beggar named Lazarus, covered with sores and longing to eat what fell from the rich man's table. Even the dogs came and licked his sores. The time came when the beggar died and the angels carried him to Abraham's side. The rich man also died and was buried. In hell, where he was in torment, he looked up and saw Abraham far away, with Lazarus by his side. So he called to him, 'Father Abraham, have pity on me and send Lazarus to dip the tip of his finger in water and cool my tongue, because I am in agony in this fire. But Abraham replied, 'Son, remember that in your lifetime you received your good things, while Lazarus received bad things, but now he is comforted here and you are in agony. And besides all this, between us and you a great chasm has been fixed, so that those who want to go from here to you cannot, nor anyone cross over from there to us.' He answered, 'Then I beg you, father, send Lazarus to my father's house, for I have five brothers. Let him warn them, so that they will not also come to this place of torment.' "Abraham replied, 'They have Moses and the Prophets; let them listen to them.' "'No, father Abraham,' he said, 'but if someone from the dead goes to them, they will repent.' "He said to him, 'If they do not listen to Moses and the Prophets, they will not be convinced even if someone rises from the dead.'"

I didn't go to the university and I don't have this much education, but because I have my eyes opened about celestial things or biblical things; I can see there are a lot of things in this story that don't make any sense at all. This doesn't hold to the road at all.

There is another important point in this story. This is that the author, who ever he is, even if he is in the Bible, asked Abraham for Lazarus, who is by Abraham's side, meaning in the camp of the living, to go warn the brothers of the bad rich man. Then, this bad rich man wanted for Lazarus, saying he is from the dead, and Abraham seemed to agree with this.

Then, how someone who is in hell, a demon condemned to hell could call Abraham; 'Father?'

Something that makes even less sense is that, Abraham, who is in the camp of the living, a friend of God could call someone in hell, a demon, 'Son?'

The author of this stupid story is saying the rich man was condemned because he had good things during his life, which is completely foolish. Which is just as bad is saying the poor is saved because he didn't have good things and had nothing but bad things in his life. To me this is a stew for cats and it is so rotten that even cats wouldn't eat it.

If the rich is condemned is it most likely for ignoring the needs of the poor, but not for having good things. No one can be saved for not having good things in this world either. There is a big chasm fixed between hell and heaven and no one can go from one place to the other, but these two had no problem communicating to each other. As far as I know, there was no internet back then.

See now what Jesus said in Matthew 12, 25. 'Every kingdom divided against itself will be ruined, and every city or household divided against itself will not stand.'

If a demon in hell tries to stop his brothers to come in, he will certainly get reprimanded by Satan. Where will he go? Believe it; the demons don't try to save anyone, not even their brothers, on the contrary.

Like I was saying, it is a story to bore you to death, but to me it is another story I used to open your eyes, to wake you up. I only hope it is working. It is one thing to invent this kind of stupid stories and it is up to everyone to believe in them or not, but it is another thing to present them to us as holy stories. I don't blame the author for inventing it; everyone is allowed to fiction, even if it is a ridicules story. I can tell he had some imagination, though I blame he or those responsible for putting it in the Holy Bible, because this is not being very smart.

See what Jesus said about Abraham in John 8, 39. ' "If you were Abraham' children," said Jesus, "then you would do the things Abraham did.'"

In another word; you wouldn't be in hell.

A member of my big family told me one day; 'The Bible, you have to take it all or not at all.'

Well, the main reason why I found all these lies, all these contradictions and the ridicules stories in the Bible is just because I took it all. The only positive fact I think it is in this story of Lazarus is the fact the demons are suffering from a flame that doesn't die and keep them in a constant torment.

Forgive my indignation. It is true that I love the Holy Scriptures, but I hate the lies and I love the truth. I certainly don't like the filthy stories of some sick men who undressed Jesus and Peter, the Messiah and the most considerate of Jesus' apostles. The attitude of the people who did this is the same attitude that Paul had and this is to tarnish Jesus' and his apostles' reputation.

The John, the true Jesus' apostle wouldn't have talked about Jesus or about himself this way. He wouldn't have said anything that makes Jesus looks like he was doing favouritism and neither make him looks like he likes men, I mean this way.

The John of Jesus, the true apostle wouldn't have said or wrote scandalous things like what is written in John 13, 23: 'The disciple Jesus loved.' And: 'Now there was leaning on Jesus' bosom one of his disciples, whom Jesus loved.'

Jesus said to love one another, but this was not to love each other the way this John and Paul seem to do.

The John of Jesus, the true one would also have talked about the death of his brother, James who was assassinated by Herod. The John of Jesus would have talked about the Jesus' transfiguration and at least something the true John lived through with his brother and Peter, for the three of them were following Jesus just about everywhere. The true John of Jesus, the apostle would have told the truth instead of stupid stories to introduce Paul in the picture. The true John of Jesus wouldn't have made Jesus a liar like the John of Paul did in John 8, 44 and John 8, 56. See John 8, 44. 'You belong to your father, the devil.' Now see John 8, 56. 'Your father Abraham rejoiced at the thought of seeing my day.'

Take note also that both verses are of the same conversation. Jesus didn't make such mistakes and he wouldn't have lied this way either.

The John of Jesus wouldn't have talked this bad against the Jews, God's people like this John of Paul did it so many times in the gospel of this John. Jesus only had one trader among his apostles and this was Judas. Don't forget there were four and five thousand men besides the women and children who were following Jesus just about everywhere. Remember, those Jesus fed? So, it is a lie to say the Jews didn't like Jesus. Ho sure, there were also the little bunch of Pharisees and scribes who didn't like to see the number of there followers getting down.

They were fighting to keep their religion going and losing some clients in their synagogues and they acted just like the leaders of the Christian churches of nowadays and of the time of Louis Riel when they found out that the truth was pulling people away from their churches. They know very well that when the truth will be known in all the nations, this will be the end for them. Don't be fooled, they too know how to read. They must have a good way to seduce, because still millions are getting caught in their traps and this even if Jesus and his disciples warned us not to be deceived. See Matthew 24, 4. 'Watch out that no one deceive you.'

The church was a business at the time of Jesus and it is a business still today. See Matthew 8, 4. 'Then Jesus said to him, "See that you don't tell anyone. But go, show yourself to the priest and offer the gift Moses commanded, as a testimony to them.'

Jesus asked this man not to tell anyone, because he too didn't want to throw himself in the mouth of the wolf. He too was not in a hurry to die.

There is another story in this gospel of John that doesn't seem to be anywhere else and this is the story of Jesus chasing the vendors out of the temple. This story contradicts and Jesus and the ancient prophets and is written in John 2, 13-16. 'And the Jews' Passover was at hand and Jesus went to Jerusalem, and found in the temple those that sold oxen and sheep and doves, and the changers of money sitting: And when he had made scourge of small cords, he drove them all out of the temple, and the sheep and the oxen; and poured out the changers' money, and overthrew the tables; and said unto them that sold doves, 'Take these things hence; make not my Father's house a house of merchandise."

No one can say the Jesus of this story is gentle either.

This is another story that was modified, I think mainly because it doesn't make any sense.

John 2, 14. 'Jesus went to Jerusalem, in the temple <u>courts</u> he found men selling cattle.'

Jesus knows God, the Father and he knows God's will and he also knows that God doesn't enter a box made by men' hands. So this means this is a different Jesus than the true Prophet who said; 'My Father's house,' in this John's story.

See now what God said about Jesus, his servant in Matthew 12, 18-19. 'Here is my servant whom <u>I have chosen</u>, the one I love, in whom I delight; I will put my Spirit on him, and he will proclaim justice to the nations. <u>He will not quarrel</u> or cry out; no one will hear his voice in the streets.

The Jesus, God's servant described in Matthew is not the same mad Jesus who is in the gospel of John who chased vendors with a whip. This is a sure thing.

Also, I don't know if I'm right or not, but it seems to me that if Jesus was born God, like the Christians say he is, God who didn't have a beginning and God called Jesus his servant instead of his son and God had to put his Spirit on his servant, just like He did with all the other prophets for him to be able to do all he was commanded, then it is false to say Jesus is God. That he is God's son like everyone who does the will of God, that he is the Prophet God has chosen to carry his word, like God Himself said it in Matthew 12, 18 and in Isaiah 42, 1-4, this makes more sense. Can we really choose our children?

The enemies of Jesus use one part of the truth to deceive, but I use, at least I try to use the whole truth to light you up. This is not quite the same. Just about everything I say or what I write about the word of God and the messages of Jesus can be verified in the Bible.

I'm finishing this book with more hymns God gave me and they were inspired to me by my love for Him and for the truth. I just know He wants me to share them with everyone.

CHAPTER 10

The Jesus' Messages

"Just remember long time ago in my journey into this world. Matthew 4, 17.
I told you everything I know about my Father's Holy Word
That I didn't come to abolish neither the law or the prophets. Matthew 5, 17.
And until all is accomplished, everything stands don't you forget. Matthew 5, 18.
I said not the smallest letter and not the least stroke of a pen. Matthew 5, 18.
None from the Law of my Father will disappear so understand. Matthew 5, 19.
But what did tell you the liar? That with my flesh onto the cross. Genesis. 3, 1 and Ephesians 2, 16.
I destroyed law and barrier, rules and commandments for the lost. Ephesians 2, 14.
One asked me what was the greatest of the commandments in the law. Matthew 22, 35-36
This was just to put me to test; he tried to find in me a flaw.
Love your God with all of your heart with all your soul and all your mind. Matthew 22, 37.
From your neighbour don't be apart Matthew 22, 39.
Follow those two and you'll be mine. Matthew 22, 40.

But what did tell you the liar? That the whole law is one command. Galates 5, 14.

And this is to love your neighbour as yourself, see now where he stands.

He doesn't speak about my Father, cause sinners too love who loves them. Matthew 5, 46.

It's good to love one another, but this won't get you to heaven.

Who's my mother? Who's my brother? Who are my sisters and my friends? Matthew 12, 48-50.

He does the will of my Father, my Father who is in heaven. Matthew 6, 9.

You are the salt of all the earth. You are the light cause you believe. Matthew 5, 13-14.

Even though sometime you get hurt, watch out for the one who deceives. Matthew 16, 24- 24, 4.

I sent you like sheep in the field through wolves so be careful for your sake. Matthew 10, 16.

And like doves have God for your shield, so therefore be shrewd as snakes.

He is clever the enemy in manipulating the truth. Genesis 3, 1-2 and Corinthians 12, 16.

He is more crafty than any, see he made Eve pick up the fruit.

So you will have for enemy for sure members of your own house. Matthew 10, 37.

You will not be worthy of me, not if you love more someone else.

To the earth then I brought the sword, so take your cross and follow me. Matthew 10, 34, 16, 24.

You won't be worthy of the Lord if you put first your family. Matthew 10, 37.

I'm the one who sowed the good seed; they are the sons of the kingdom. Matthew 13, 37-38.

My enemy who sowed the weeds and they all are the devil's sons. Matthew 13, 38-39.

One day I will send my angels to through the weeds in the furnace. Matthew 13, 41-42.

There will be then no more rebels, you'll shine like the sun in this place. Matthew 13, 41-43.

Just remember long time ago in my journey into this world. Matthew 4, 17.

I told you everything I know about my Father's Holy Word That I didn't come to abolish neither the law or the prophets. Matthew 5, 17.

And until all is accomplished, everything stands don't you forget. Everything stands don't you forget. Matthew 5, 18.

Praises To My Lord

I want to sing praises to my Lord with the angels,
With the angels of heaven.
And I want to be happy up there
With the angels and Adam, Eve and Abel.
I want to sing praises to my Lord
With the angels, with the angels of heaven
And I want to be happy up there
With the angels and with all of his children
1-6
Listening to Jesus, to Jesus and Moses,
This is how I have known the Father as my own
And because they told me, this is why I can see.
Yes now I can see through and I believe the truth.
2
I'll be able to meet the great Job and Jacob
Shake hands with Abraham, I am one of his fans.
I don't need Cadillac to meet with Isaac.
I'll sing with the angels, Daniel and Ezekiel.
3
I will seal with Noah and walk with Jeremiah
I'll fish with Hosea also with Isaiah.
I will build some mentions with David and Samson.
Be with the apostles and Jesus' disciples.
4
My heart is with Joseph who in prison was kept.
Was like me a dreamer didn't want to be sinner.
So my God was with him, kept him away from sin.
I'll meet him when ever there at the Lord supper.
5
Now's the great gathering, will you be there to sing
With all of us one day in the heavens to pray?
The Lord is powerful. He's with whom is faithful.
He will not let you down, come join us in the round.

6

Listening to Jesus, to Jesus and Moses,
This is how I have known the Father as my own
And because they told me, this is why I can see.
Yes now I can see through and I believe the truth.
Chorus
I want to sing praises to my Lord with the angels,
With the angels of heaven.
And I want to be happy up there
With the angels and Adam, Eve and Abel.
I want to sing praises to my Lord
With the angels, with the angels of heaven
And I want to be happy up there
With the angels and with all of his children.

Alone At Christmas.

I was alone the night of this Christmas.
When someone came knocking at the door.
He said sir what are you crying for?
Ain't it the time to be happy?
Would you let me in out of your kindness?
I assure you that my feet are sore.
And I don't mind to sleep on the floor,
As long as you feel safe with me.

I said my friend my house is a real mess.
I basically have nothing to eat.
All I can give you is a place to rest.
Come by the stove and warm up your feet."
2
"All I have on are nothing but old rags.
Don't have enough to cover my skin.
And the soles of my shoes are so thin.
I wondered how I could survive.
All I own I carry in my old bag.
An old picture of my aged mother.
A pocket knife, bar soap, opener.
Amazing that I'm still alive."

"I'll see what I have left in my cupboards.
I have spaghetti, macaroni.
All I have to put on, salt and pepper.
And for dessert it's peanut butter."
3
"Well I had nothing to eat for three days.
I can't afford to be too fussy.
It's been long since I had spaghetti.
Would you please sir make one for me?"

"My friend I had nobody in for years.
Just sit down, and I'll make us supper.
If it's right we'll eat it together.
And then we'll have a sing along."

"I can see that you are a musician.
And you have all those nice instruments.
I have dreamed to become a physician.
But what I do is more important."
Spoken part

"How could you walk among all my dogs without alarming them? It is basically impossible to do." "They must have known that I was harmless. They are pretty smart too." "I know the Lord said He would come back like a thief; that no one knows the day or the hour." "The thieves are harmful, the Lord is bountiful." "How come you didn't eat for three days? There are a lot of good people out there." "Well, the church was closed and there was nobody around. The door was locked and there is no shelter in this little town." "How could you survive the nights in such a cold?" "I sneaked into barns and I slept in a doghouse one night with a big old malamute that gave me a lot of heat." "It wasn't one of mine, was it?" "No, it was miles away." "Well, I don't have much, but you can stay here for as long as you wish." "You have plenty; just try to carry what you own in a pack sac." "I have sweaters, shirts, pans and shoes that I don't wear anymore. You are welcome to take what you need. I also have a brand new bag that is better and bigger than yours. It is strange that you are exactly the same size as I am." "I can't take too much; this wouldn't help me with my mission." "What is your ministry?" "I test people's hearts for my Lord." "I minister with my songs, my music and my writing. That's why I need all of those instruments." "I know; that's why I'm here. I have this one song the Lord wants you to sing along. It's called;

Alone at Christmas and it goes like this.

He was alone the night of this Christmas. When someone came knocking at his door. He said sir, what are you crying for? Ain't it a time to be happy? Would you let me in out of your kindness? I assure you that my feet are sore. And I don't mind to sleep on the floor, as long as you feel safe with me.

As long as you feel safe with me.

Tonight

Tonight if my God is willing.
Tonight, you'll know of my feelings.
Tonight I'll put my head to rest.
And I will lay it on your breast. (chest)
I have been waiting for so long.
To hear from you, to tell me too.
I wrote it in my books and songs,
How much I love and I want you.
Chorus; How much he loves and he wants you.
Tonight we'll start a brand new life,
To lead us through eternity.
Tonight we'll be husband and wife,
The golden path is so pretty.
It's for us two that I believed,
In our love, in our destiny.
For this reason we will receive,
All the blessings He promised me.
Chorus; All the blessings He promised thee.
Tonight you'll be for my own eye,
The tree of life, the tree of joy
Tonight we'll be for you and I,
The root of pleasure to enjoy
My Lord has shown me how to reach,
The very deepness of your soul
The kind of love for me to teach,
This one is to fulfill his goal.
Chorus: This one is to fulfill his goal.
Tonight if my God is willing.
Tonight, you'll know of my feelings.
Tonight I'll put my head to rest.
And I will lay it on your breast.
Chorus; And he will lay it on your breast, tonight.

In My Dreams, You're Mine

When I lay down alone at night, you're on my mind.
And when I wake in the morning, you're in my mind.
There in between, there in my dreams, I know you're mine.
But all day long, I walk alone in the meantime.
Course
He; Precious Princess, I know that you are the dearest.
She; My charming Prince, you know now that I am convinced.
You're my soul mate; I have no doubt, for I have faith.
It is the Lord, Who worked this out, it is our fate.
2
For all of the eternity one we will be.
There is a plan, a destiny for you and me.
For what my God has united, no one separates.
There's a mansion, He has prepared for us to take.
Course
He; Precious Princess, I know that you are the dearest.
She; My charming Prince, you know now that I am convinced.
You're my soul mate; I have no doubt, for I have faith.
It is the Lord, Who worked this out, it is our fate.
3
When I lay down alone at night, you're on my mind.
And when I wake in the morning, you're in my mind.
There in between, there in my dreams, I know you're mine.
But all day long, I walk alone in the meantime.
I'll walk alone in the meantime.

The Shining Star

The star, five of us, together formed tonight should shine forever and ever.

It points as you can see in every direction that means to all of the nations.

You are Swedish and I am French. She is Polish, he is German.

We speak English, we understand even if she is Italian.

Let's go out and form some more stars like this one, some stars that will shine just like ours.

To light the world from living in this darkness. This is what the Lord wants from us. Matthew 5, 14.

To plant the seed, pull out the weeds, find the good soil, do it with joy.

Make a garden, food of heaven, form some more stars that shine afar. Mat: 28, 20.

Instrumental

We have to tell the best of news. Jesus is here, don't be confused. Matthew 4, 17.

From East to West, the world will see. He is the best, he sets you free. Matthew 24, 27.

This star that will shine like the sun, Jesus said in the kingdom of our Father. Matthew 13, 43.

And then we will sit there with him on the throne happy to finally be at home.

Happy to finally be at home.

He Was Only a Man

He was nothing, but he was fair, was nobody.
Who did something, for his people, he was a man.
Was elected, was evicted fought all the way.
His victory, our history, the guy has wan.
A patriot, strong wills fighter, a Canadian.
Gave his best shot as a worker until the end
Recognition, form the nation is essential.
Cause with his life, he paid the price, this was Riel.
Course
Riel, you're a hero; now lot of people know
That you were innocent, for the crime you were sent
Riel, you're a hero, now lot of people know,
You didn't deserve to die, this way under the sky.
Riel, you're a hero, now lot of people know
That your cause is not lost, it's heard and it's a most.
Riel, you're the hero, now lot of people know
I told many of them, your home is the Heavens. Mat.
5, 10.
2
And he had faith, this Canadian until the end.
In his country who betrayed him and all his friends.
Will he be paid, for all the aid he contributed?
For the rights of, Metes and whites, Native's disputes
His sacrificed most of his life for the settlers
It would be nice, to see his rights for the others.
It's not in vain; he fought the shame it's our glory.
His cause today, democracy, our victory
Course
Riel, you're a hero; now lot of people know
That you were innocent, for the crime you were sent
Riel, you're a hero, now lot of people know,
You didn't deserve to die, this way under the sky.
Riel, you're a hero, now lot of people know

That your cause is not lost, it's heard and it's a most.
Riel, you're the hero, now lot of people know
I told many of them, your home is the Heavens
I told many of them, your home is the Heavens. Mat.
5, 10.

Everything's Yours Oh Lord

Everything's yours oh Lord.
My heart, my soul, my life.
All my sufferings, I put within your hands.
I understand. You are the Counselor.
The Mighty Lord of all.
You see my heart in tears.
You know about my fears.
You know that I'm sincere and I love You.
Almighty Lord of all.
I have known so much joy.
Now everything's destroyed.
Give me back to enjoy, a love life too.
2
Oh come and help me Lord, of the impossible.
Once You have changed the heart of a lion
Unto a fawn's
And You are the healer.
Oh Mighty Lord of all
If it's against your will
I know that You can heal
My heart seriously ill, easy for You
Almighty Lord of all.
Listen to my prayer.
I know You can tell her
Cause all of the power, belongs to You
Second part spoken and back to first and end.

Precious Princess of Wonderland

1

Welcome to Wonderland to you Precious Princess.
You've accepted the Lord, the Lord accepted you.
Now you're here in his land and forever you'll rest.
What you're seeing is for you, cause you've believed the truth.
This is the Promised Land given us by the Lord
Pure water and white sand, you will never be bored
All you will ever need is here for you to take
All those beautiful things were put there for your sake

2

You will never get hurt, you will never get scared
All the bad of the earth got caught in Jesus' care
You'll never be hungry, and you will never thirst
Forever be happy, cause you put Jesus first
Forever and ever you're a child of our King
Come to the Lord's supper, He'll tell you everything
And He'll give you the crown, you deserve all around
All the diamonds, the gold, the rubies and the pearls

3

Then you can sing with us to princes and princesses
Whom have carried their cross so now too they can rest
Others have washed their robes in the blood of the Lamb
Let us welcome them all to this beautiful land
For the eternity you'll have immunity
No one can take away what it is yours to stay
The bad have been destroyed nothing is left but joy
Peace and love all the way, promised milk and honey

Part spoken

Will you sing with us to the princes and princesses?
Will you carry your cross so you too can rest?
Did you wash your robe in the blood of the Lamb?
Will you be welcome in this beautiful land?

Will you have immunity for the eternity?
Will you have all those things no one can take away?
Will you be destroyed with the bad or live forever in joy?
Will you live in peace and love all the way with milk and honey?

1 and 4

Welcome to Wonderland to you, Precious Princess
You've accepted the Lord, the Lord accepted you
Now you're here in his land and forever you'll rest
What you're seeing is for you, cause you believed the truth
What you're seeing is for you, cause you believed the truth.

The Final Warning

Listen to this one great news sent to you today
To me it's the greatest; the Lord is on his way
He has made the universe, the earth and heavens
And all that you can see has been made by his hands
'Many times I have showed you the mighty power
I have flooded the earth, but I have saved Noah
When Abram the good man had pleaded for his friends
They got out of the towns Sodom and Gomorrah
2
Do you remember Joseph I sent to exile?
He was sold by his brothers, he was put in jail
He was to save my people from the starvation
Of a deadly famine seven years duration
And what to say of Moses drew out of water?
To guide you through the crises and lots of danger
I told him all I wanted as for you to know
He carried all my commands down to you below
3
The wisdom of Solomon, the strength of Samson.
Can just not save your soul from the lake of fire
Only Jesus the Saviour with his compassion
Left his beautiful home, they took him for ransom
I sent you my beloved Son for the sacrifice
He has done nothing wrong yet he has paid the price
Now if you are telling Me, this is not for you
Just one more thing to say, I've done all I can do
Instrumental
4
Now you are out of time and I am out of blood
Too many of my children have died for their God
Many of Jesus' good friends and his apostles
And so many others died as his disciples
Now it is time to crown My Own Beloved Son

He's going back to run everything that I've done
Will you be lost forever or will you be saved?
This is what you should know before you hit the grave!'
5
Listen to this one great news sent to you today
To me it's the greatest the Lord is on his way
He has made the universe, the earth and heavens
And all that you can see has been made by his hands
And all that you can see has been made by his hands.

For better or worse

For better or worse always and forever
That's what my love is for you
For ever are yours all my heart and my soul
My love will always be true

The kind that does come from above, Compassion and Fidelity, Cleaner and purer than a dove, I'll love you through eternity
2
For all of my life, all my days and my nights, for you I'll always be right.
Through good and bad times, through the storms and sunshine
Always you'll see my love shine.

The kind that does come from above
Compassion and Fidelity,
Cleaner and purer than a dove,
I'll love you through eternity.
3
When this life's over, when I've done what I could
I'll go to a much better world
There I will enter where there is no suffer,
A home made for me by the Lord

In this home I will reach above, awesome gift from Fidelity,
The One who is nothing but love, Master of the eternity
4
For better or worse, always and forever,
His love for all of us too
Forever are yours all his grace and his peace
His love will always be true

The King who did come from above,
Compassion and Fidelity
So clean and so pure is his love
With us for the eternity
5
For better or worse, always and forever
That's what his love is for you. Forever are yours all
My heart and my soul, my love will always be true
The love that does come from above,
Compassion and Fidelity
So clean and so pure is his love,
With us for the eternity.'

The Smell of Roses

Thank You my Lord, thank You my Lord, thank You my Lord.
1
Thank You my Lord for this wonderful smell of roses
Thank You my Lord for giving me so many things
Is it for us time of the apotheosis?
It's time for me to say thank You for great blessings

I know You are the Almighty
You have made this beautiful flower just for me
She is faded, as You can see
Only You can bring her back to what she used to be

We are the seed, the garden of your kingdom
Your creation made by your hands, your ambition
Your enemy, yes this despicable phantom
He has faded my nice flower, my companion

God You blessed us and You told us. Genesis 1, 28!
'To be fruitful, to multiply, fill up the earth
To rule over, birds in the sky,
Fish in the sea and everything upon the earth'

Thank You my Lord for this wonderful smell of roses
Thank You my Lord for giving me so many things
Is it for us time of the apotheosis?
It's time for me to say thank You for great blessings
Thank You my Lord for making me as your likeness.

Only One is Holy

Only, only, only, One is Holy, Holy, Holy
He is the Almighty
Funny, funny, funny, so many are called holy
When Jesus said that only One is good. Mat:19-16
Spoken
And then he wasn't even talking about himself, but about the
Father in heaven, the One he served faithfully and loved dearly

Today, today, today, I know about what's holy
The truth revealed to me
The truth from Almighty, this was Jesus' delivery
The true prophet, the one hanged on the wood
Spoken
He didn't do it for the money, or for gold
He didn't do it for a religion, or for an empire
He did for the Father and for us,
Whom he loved more than his own live
This was Jesus the true prophet of God, who was the king
Of the Jews in the year 30-33 of our time. He was crowned
With thorns when he deserved all the richest of this world.
Follow his word and you will enter the kingdom of heaven
While still on earth, because if you do, you'll never die
Matthew 19, 17
His word, which means, God the Father will hold you from
Falling into the abomination that causes spiritual death
Be free from the slavery of sins and experience the total happiness.

This was Jesus' and is my wish for you.

Only, only, only, One is Holy, Holy, Holy.
He is the Almighty.
Funny, funny, funny, so many are called holy.
When Jesus said that only One is good.
Yes Jesus said that only One is good. Mat:19-16-17.

On Whose Side Are You?

Will you be on the side of Jesus?
Will you be on the side of the one?
Who sacrificed his life so we can get a life;
The one who tells the truth that hid from you the enemy?
Will you be on the side of Jesus?
Will you be on the side of the one?
Who was killed on the cross,
The one that we can trust
He gave his life for us;
All what he said is true, not like the enemy.
Will you be on the side of Jesus?
Will you be on the side of the one?
Who made you the promise, you will see liveliness
When you will be accused and
Then you won't be confused by the enemy?
Will you be on the side of Jesus?
Will you be on the side of the one?
Who said to be careful when the beast will be awful;
You will have to flee away
When you are persecuted by the enemy
Will you be on the side of Jesus?
Will you be on the side of the one?
When he'll come back to get
All the ones who didn't forget,
The ones he'll put on his right,
On the other side his enemy
I know that I am on Jesus' side
I know I'm on the side of the one;
The one who told me the truth,
He was killed for the same truth,
But we'll win over the enemy
Yes I am on the side of Jesus.

I love My Neighbour As Myself

Part sang
I love my neighbour as myself, that causes me some problems
What can you do when you're turned down trying to help someone?
Part spoken
I walked into a restaurant the other day and a man say hi to me.
I said hi too and I told him to go ahead even though I was in first.
He said; 'No, you go ahead, I have all day.' I said ok then,
I'll bet you that this girl can serve two coffees at the same time and she did.
So when came to pay, I paid for both and he said;
'No, you don't buy me coffee.' Almost in madness!
'You owe me nothing and I owe nothing.' And he put a toony ($2) in the tray.
So I took a loony ($1.) and I gave it to him, thinking;
If you can't take it, it's because you can't give.
Part sang
I love my neighbour as myself that causes me some problems
What can you do when you're turned down trying to help someone?
Second part spoken
There's a young woman whom I like who works in the same place and I saw her limping with sore feet. I know she's working seven days a week trying to make ends meet. So I wrote in a napkin that seeing her suffer is killing me and I put some money in it, asking her to buy a good pair of shoes, because I want her to be comfortable when she walks up to my table. She brought it back all

upset telling me that she couldn't take it. I felt so sad thinking; if you can't take it's because you can't give.

Part sang

I love my neighbour as myself, which causes me some problems

What can you do when you're turned down trying to help someone?

3rd part spoken

A man I know came to fix my driveway the same day and he did a very good job. So I gave him a little more than he had expected. Then he handed me back forty dollars, saying;

'It's more than I deserve.' I took twenty dollars out of his hand telling him; I'll share it with you if you like it better, but then again, I couldn't help thinking, if you can't take it, it's because you can't give.

Part sang

I love my neighbour as myself, that causes me some problems

What can you do when you're turned down trying to help someone?

4th part spoken

At the end of that day I was filled with sadness thinking of Jesus who left everything behind to give us the word of God, God who talked to him as he walked day by day! He gave much more than I could ever give, by healing the sick, bringing back to life and mainly opening the eyes of the blind!

Through all of his ministry he risked his life every minute of every day until they took it. How many still today say; 'Thanks but no thanks? I can't take it.' They can't take it, I think because they can't give. Today someone gave me an extra dollar and I knew it was from the heart. I gladly took it, because I love to give.

Part sang

I love my neighbour as myself that causes me some problems
What can you do when you're turned down trying to help someone? Trying to help someone?

You Told Me Lord

You told me oh my Lord; You brought to us the sword
The kingdom of heaven belongs to your children
You made beautiful things, for You I'll be pleading
I found You amazing and for You I will sing

You are the Father of the heavens and the earth
You know all the secrets of the earth and the see
Some want to take over what you created first
Only You knows how to control the universe

Only You know to change our heart and our thoughts
What can I do for You? For You I love so much
From your word came my faith, now I do know my fate
For You I want to sing, the Master of all things

You are the Father of the heavens and the earth
You know all the secrets of the earth and the see
Some want to take over what you created first
Only You knows how to control the universe

You showed me oh my Lord that life is not a game
Many mock you my Lord, everywhere is the shame
Everything goes down hill, enough to make me ill
Sing is my destiny for the eternity

You are the Father of the heavens and the earth
You know all the secrets of the earth and the see
Some want to take over what you created first
Only You knows how to control the universe
Only You knows how to control the universe.

Some people will say that I am out of balance just because I have one leg just a bit shorter than the other one. They will also find a reason to eliminate me instead of illuminate me. I am kind of happy we passed the time of burning people like me alive on the stake, but I am not out of these threats yet anyway. Although no one can say I wasn't aware of the risks I am in by writing the way I do or the things I'm writing about. There was a very good reason why the Jesus' apostles and his disciples were hiding to meet and to pray.

There was a very good reason too why Jesus told them to wait for him in Galilee, on the mountain Jesus told them to go. See Matthew 28, 16. 'Then the eleven disciples went to Galilee, to the mountain where Jesus had told them to go.'

Paul and the Romans were extremely dangerous for Jesus' disciples then and for what I know; they are not less dangerous today. Although most of the apostles knew it, at least according to what is written in Acts 9, 1. 'Meanwhile, Saul (Paul) was still breathing out murderous threats against the Lord's disciples.'

See also Acts 8, 1. 'On that day a great persecution broke out against the church of Jerusalem and all except the apostles were scattered throughout Judea and Samaria.'

From this day on the Gentiles began to know about the truth and some of them are the ones who knew enough to argued against Paul's teaching.

Jesus told his apostles not to enter the towns of Samaria, see Matthew 10, 5-6. 'These twelve Jesus sent out with the following instructions: "Do not go among the Gentiles or enter any town of the Samaritans. Go rather to the lost sheep of Israel.'

See Acts 8, 3. 'But Saul (Paul) began to destroy the church. Going from house to house, he dragged men and women and put them in prison.'

See Acts 8, 4. 'Those who had been scattered preached the word wherever they went.'

Those, my friends are the ones who told the truth to the Gentiles and argued against those who were lying like Paul and his disciples.

What most people don't seem to know is that Paul is even more dangerous today than he was then. He has a lot more followers nowadays than then. He was attacking people' s bodies back then, now with the help of his successors, his imitators he is attacking people's souls by shutting down in their faces the access of the kingdom of heaven, just like Jesus said it. See again Matthew 23, 13. 'But woe to you, scribes and Pharisees, hypocrites, (priests, bishops, archbishops, cardinals, popes and pastors and all of Paul's products) because you shut off the kingdom of heaven from people, for you don't enter it yourselves, nor do you allow those who are entering to go in.'

Paul learned enough from the prisoners, the Jesus' disciples with torturing them and who knows what else, to be able to infiltrate them; which I would call; the wolf in the sheep pen. Jesus called this; 'The parable of the weeds.'

You might say that I am often repeating myself, but to me, some things can't be repeated often enough, especially when this concerns the seducer who forbids you to see the truth, to see the kingdom of heaven.

So I wish you good luck, but luck you will gain it the day you will put the liar and his lies out of your life and by accepting Jesus' messages, by accepting the truth.

From James Prince, a Jesus' disciple who loves the true God with all of his heart, his soul and his mind.

If someone is interested to receive a cassette or a Cd of my songs, he can communicate with me at: **jamesprince@sasktel.net**.

I will also be available to discuss with anyone who looks for a civilized debate, a civilized discussion. James Prince.